CW01032922

JANE DE TELIGA is a fashion writer, editor, stylist, and curator. Ever since she was a little girl Jane has adored fashion and travel. It all began when her grandmother Kath bought her a fine panama boater trimmed in pale pink organza flowers and took her on a memorable train trip from Sydney to Adelaide.

Working for a couple of decades for leading magazines and newspapers around the world, she has reported on the fashion collections in London, Paris and Milan. She has been the Style Director of *The Australian Women's Weekly*, Australia's best loved magazine; Fashion Features Editor-at-large on *Harper's Bazaar Australia*; and Style and Fashion Editor of *The Sydney Morning Herald*.

After a life-changing decision, she packed two suitcases and moved to Europe. Since then she has worked for *The Australian* newspaper as European Fashion correspondent and been Fashion Director of *Good Housekeeping* in the UK, and is currently Senior Lecturer of Fashion Styling at Southampton Solent University.

You can find her on the web at janedeteliga.com

Running Away FROM HOME

FINDING A NEW LIFE IN PARIS, LONDON AND BEYOND

JANE DE TELIGA

LANTERN

an imprint of
PENGUIN BOOKS

THIS PAGE
*Home and away: Bronte beach,
so close to home.*

RIGHT
*Work and play on the balcony
of Hôtel de Crillon, Paris.*

CHAPTER ONE

How I came to RUN AWAY

BY AIR MAIL
PAR AVION

*

Leaving Sydney and my empty nest

One dreary, sad winter's day I found myself at Sydney's unprepossessing international airport, two suitcases in hand, clutching my beautiful daughter Emily, struggling to breathe as I said goodbye to everything. The enormity of what I was doing was shimmering like a mirage somewhere at the back of my brain. 'Let's pretend I'm just going on holidays,' I croaked, 'I just can't say goodbye.' And weaving their way through that brain mirage in big letters were the words, 'What the fuck are you doing, Jane! You're leaving your girls! The most important thing in your life! You're leaving your family, your friends, your job and your home. Are you completely bloody crazy?'

After a final clutch I made a strangled dash into the immigration hall. A middle-aged, middle-class Australian woman in her comfy velour tracksuit pants struggling to regain her composure, basically making a run for it; a run towards a new life.

Let's backtrack, but let me caution you first. This is my story, as honest as I can make it, about what happened when I decided to create a new life for myself. The innate narcissism of telling my story confronts me at every turn, but here goes.

People who hear my story always say, 'You're so brave!' or 'How courageous'. But bravery had nothing to do with it. My decision to pull the rug out from under my own feet and move to the other side of the world was more about saving my own life. It was about finding a life that I chose, rather than a life that chose me.

This is the part where I say, 'I had it all'. Well, yes, I did but I didn't. A pretty little cottage in the eastern suburbs of Sydney, ten minutes from the beach, the smell of sweet jasmine wafting on a warm night, a palm tree swishing in the breeze in my tiny courtyard – my home. There are memories of hanging out the clothes in the backyard, naked, on a blistering hot day ('For godsake Mum put some clothes on.'), lying in bed snuggling up with my daughters, Emily and Mads, on either side in 'a mummy sandwich', catching up with each other's news, late at night in the still air, hearing the distant roar of the surf rolling in on

Bright shiny day: Sydney Heads from Watson's Bay on a dazzling Sydney afternoon.

TOP
*Family portrait: Emily, me and
Madeleine in Sydney, 2010.*

BOTTOM
*Kookaburra sits on old goal post,
Waverley.*

Bronte Beach, walking through the bush gully on a sunny day, the spicy scent of eucalyptus in the air, heading down to the sparkling sea and diving into the cool, salty water. My annual birthday drinks, the only entertaining I ever seemed to manage, were held in a gardenia-scented courtyard on a summer night, full of the hum of laughing and chatting friends. There was much time spent nattering for hours with my dear friend Alexandra over a cup of herbal tea, at her place or mine, or going to dinner down the road at my mother's place; a woman who must be the best home cook in the world, just as her mother Kath was before her. These were just a few of my favourite things.

But until you've experienced the empty-nest syndrome you will probably wonder what the problem was. My two lovely girls, who I had lived with, nurtured and annoyed, shouted at and laughed with, sung and danced with (when they would let me) for more than twenty years, grew up. Those beautiful, maddening, wonderful, so clever, so funny lights of my life – tra la la, they went to university, my old alma mater Sydney University. Emily to do an economics (social sciences) degree followed by a law degree, Madeleine taking on media and communications. They both did so well with very little help from me and I am immensely proud of them. They found really lovely boyfriends, Emily's Adrian and Madeleine's Tim, both indie rock musicians (I think it must have been a childhood of watching *Countdown*, *en famille*, every Sunday night). Then each of these gorgeous girls left home for good, leaving me to wander up and down the hallway wondering why life suddenly felt so empty. And I pined (as in 'That parrot's not dead, it's pining for the fjords', to quote *Monty Python*), and I was alone.

It's not that I lacked a social life – being in the public eye as a prominent fashion person meant I was invited to anything and everything that was happening in Sydney. Much of my social life was bound up with my job. Launches, parties, dinners, first nights, but it suddenly seemed that it was all about what I did rather than who I really was.

I did have a small group of wonderful friends that I loved, who loved me and they were and still are so precious to me. But the truth was that I had never really been alone before. People have always surrounded me.

I grew up in a big crazy family and there were always people around, not just my own family but all our friends and extended family as well – 'the whole catastrophe' to quote *Zorba the Greek*. There was my father, John, a difficult but brilliant man and my gregarious, hospitable mother, Rae. Being the eldest of six children (the biblical-sounding Andrew, Sarah, Matthew (now dead), Martha and Emma), I was used to a life surrounded by others and with our family there was always a swirling emotional life with nary a dull moment. Arguments, political polemic, loud music, creativity, love and anger and dramas of all kinds – it was the whole world in microcosm. Even now my mother continues to be the centre of our family life and we all continue to orbit around her, not only her own children but all her grandchildren too.

To add to my 'aloneness', I was single for the first time in a very long time. From my mid teens onwards, there had always been a steady stream of long-term boyfriends with years together and small breaks in between one and another. Then, at twenty-eight, I married a lovely man, who also came from another big family. Somewhere in the craziness of juggling our careers (fashion and coal mining are not exactly compatible!) and having two children and commuting back and forth from a tiny coastal town, we eventually lost our way. And after twelve years together we divorced, which was a nasty shock to the system.

From then on I was a single mother in a life so busy I could hardly breathe. I was juggling an ambitious media career and motherhood, and doing it very badly with all the attendant guilt and exhaustion. Who told us that you could have it all?

In between all of this, as the children were growing up, I was also juggling my not so successful personal life. Amongst some of the disastrous entanglements was a tortuous five-year long on-and-off relationship with a charismatic but troubled man. A man who I remained hooked to, through his searing highs and lows, by a line with a breaking strain fit for a whale. After one little lie too many from him, the line finally and miraculously snapped and I was free. But free to do what?

I still had my all-consuming job as Style Director on the Australian publishing icon, *The Australian Women's Weekly*. And it had taken up eight full-on years of my life while my girls were growing up. Being the style director meant that my working life involved organising, creating and directing the photographic images that enlivened the magazine. It was like being a film director or the conductor of an orchestra. It meant coming up with the concept and then, with teams of fantastically creative people, bringing that concept to life, shooting some of Australia's most fascinating people – famous, sometimes infamous and sometimes completely unknown people. Each shoot would begin with a kernel of an idea in my head (okay a bit *Ab Fab* 'I see sky . . .'). It could start in my mind with anything from a colour, a gown, a song title that would morph, via the creative talents of many people, into the full-blown photograph shoots you see on the cover and the stories inside the magazine. You can't imagine how much work and how many people go into making a great photo sing. For me, it involved flying around the country, directing shoots with everybody from supermodels to everyday people, television stars to Olympians, not to mention the odd Academy award winner. It gave me extraordinary access to Australia and the high profile and down-to-earth ordinary people who shape this country.

I've done shoots with every prime minister or would-be prime minister in recent years. I've sat and had tea with Julia Gillard and her fine, welcoming parents at their home in Adelaide, long before she became prime minister. I remember being so impressed with her father, a soft-spoken Welshman with serious, reasoned principles, when we discussed corruption in the Olympics. I've styled and directed a shoot with Julia and her partner Tim, lounging on the lawn at Vaucluse House, when we first started hearing about her and was

TOP
*Style director at work: Me styling
a shoot about celebrity stylists for the*
Australian Women's Weekly.
Photo: Juli Balla

BOTTOM
*Cover story: Beside one of my
Christmas covers of Megan Gale.*

Photo: Clementine O'Hara

impressed by what a nice couple they were. I've visited Kirribilli House to direct a shoot with the then Prime Minister John Howard and his wife, Janette, at the front door, asking him put his arm around his wife (I had *American Gothic* in my head) to try and make it all seem a bit friendlier. I've hung out at home on the Perth porch with a genial Kim Beazley and his wife Susie, in his run-up to a major election, and been on a shoot on the tropical Brisbane porch of Kevin Rudd with his impressive wife, Therese, and children just after he became prime minister for the first time.

I've done many shoots with the luscious Megan Gale as a shimmering golden angel and in a glamorous red bow dress for Christmas covers with the lovely photographer Graham Shearer, as well as shooting her and her Italian boyfriend of the time in a stunning villa overlooking Lago Maggiore in Italy before heading off to Hayman Island to style her as a Polynesian princess, with the easy-going Graham shooting again. With Chris Colls, we shot Megan on the dazzling white sands and red rocks of Broome for a fashion shoot. And with the ebullient Gary Heery, we even shot Megan with an elephant in an echo of Richard Avedon's famous 1950s shot in a series we did with well-known Australians and zoo animals. (Did you know you cannot separate one elephant from the herd or they all get distressed, so you have to have the whole herd in proximity?) For the same series we shot the innately elegant Ian Thorpe at the zoo with a magnificent giraffe.

I've directed shoots with countless other famous swimmers from the easy-going Susie O'Neill (who didn't blink when I stupidly asked her what kind of swimming she did, when all of Australia knew her as 'Madame Butterfly') to Kieran Perkins and his then wife Symantha at home. I spent time with cricketer Glen McGrath and his pretty English wife Jane, creating a beautiful shoot of them at their waterfront home, a year or so before she died from breast cancer.

I've flown to the personal zoo of Steve Irwin after his death and been with his grieving wife Terri, their irrepressible daughter Bindi and little son Robert, along with a whole herd of majestic elephants (who speak only Burmese), and some scary-looking crocodiles (mute and very sinister). I still remember the sight of a tiny Bindi in a bright pink tutu, standing in front of a massive elephant, singing while it swayed in time to her song.

With my dear friend, the most stylish photographer in the world, Juli Balla, we shot countless covers of television personalities and actresses (I refuse to use that silly unisex term 'actor'), including the beautiful shots of Lisa McCune (still one of my favourite shots), Kerry Armstrong, Toni Collette and Megan Gale, again, to name a few.

I've flown to London to do a shoot of the flame-haired Duchess of York by photographer James Houston, after yet another of her ill-fated escapades (one of the many I have done since with the Duchess). I've done shoots with the delightful Sarah Murdoch in Sydney, including one beautiful shot as a 1930s movie star by Jez Smith, and a gorgeous *Australian Women's Weekly* cover by Hugh Stewart of Sarah in a delicious blue Lanvin dress. I've flown to Los Angeles to work with the mercurial Rachel Griffiths and songstress Olivia Newton-John at home.

While I had extraordinary access to the powerful, famous and infamous in my working life, the currency of celebrity was never a huge deal to me, it was simply my job. Not that I took it all for granted, it was fascinating to meet the people who were being talked about. Some people I loved, some I didn't and not always the expected ones. I took that access as seriously as I took on the notion of professional confidentiality. But ultimately my priority, my obsession in fact, was getting good images. People would often ask me for gossip and I was of little use on that front; most of what I saw and heard disappeared as soon as I had the shots in the bag. But who could forget the wonderful Dame Elisabeth Murdoch, who took us on a tour of her home in Victoria and reminisced about her son Rupert's childhood and then sat down to have lunch with us; a delicious, simple meal that included her own home-grown raspberries. Or hanging out in a hotel with the affable and friendly Hugh Jackman in a bathrobe (him not me) between shots. What's not to love about that?

God, my working life was marvellous but after nearly eight years – hello burnout. Plucking ideas from my head, creating a concept and making it happen with a fantastic photographer and team was the best job anyone could have had and I loved it. But it finally wore me out, plundering my brain of every creative idea. In the end, it refused to cough up anything any more and I realised I needed some serious rebooting for myself and for new inspiration. Europe was the place that beckoned.

My last cover shoot for the *Australian Women's Weekly* was the beautiful gold cover with Nicole Kidman in Los Angeles, who was utterly charming, warm and friendly, nothing like the cool diva of people's pre-conceptions. She wore two specially made gold goddess dresses created by Collette Dinnigan, which she chose from design sketches we presented. The shoot with American photographer James White was beautiful. Afterwards, at Nicole's request, I went on to style her for a film shoot for a Nintendo Brain Training campaign with a stills shoot by the legendary Patrick Demarchelier. (The film and stills were shown all over Europe.) I had dinner with Nicole, Patrick and the team after it all wrapped. That was my last big shoot in Sydney – what a way to end 'my brilliant career'.

Around that time my long-time friend, Linda Slutzkin, died. We had worked together at The Art Gallery of New South Wales when I was a junior curator; we had brought up our children together and continued seeing each other. Linda was one of those life enhancers, so generous, throwing great parties with her partner Albie Thoms, full of family and swags of old radicals and talented 'creatives' from art and film. The last time we ever talked was when I visited her in the hospice. I had just been to Paris where I had lit a candle for her in Notre Dame. When I told her I'd just got back from Paris, she whispered

WW|fashion

*On the beach: The sublime Broome shoot
with Megan Gale and Chris Colls.*
Photo (right): Chris Colls

Megan drifts
dreamily on Cable
Beach wearing
gorgeous centre
dyed chiffon
in delicious
sorbet colours.
Alex Perry silk
chiffon dress, $2500.
Jan Logan quartz
earrings, $275.

THE AUSTRALIAN
Women's Weekly

ROYAL SHOCK TACTICS
Princess Caroline teaches her young son a lesson

FERGIE CONFESSES
"I'm still fighting the fat lady inside me"

INTIMATE INTERVIEW
Julia Gillard shows off the man in her life

OUR FARMERS FIND LOVE
11 marriages, 9 engagements and 8 babies!

THE NEW RULES OF DATING FOR EVERY AGE

Easy Entertaining
• Celebrity dinner party menus
• Mouthwatering chocolate recipes

PLUS
ARE YOU AN EMOTIONAL EATER? TAKE OUR QUIZ

EXCLUSIVE
SARAH MURDOCH
A RARE GLIMPSE INTO HER PRIVATE WORLD

SHREK BONUS: 8 FUN-FILLED PAGES OF GAMES AND PUZZLES

Women's Weekly

WILLIAM AT 25
Why Diana would not be happy

BEAUTY & THE BEAST STAR
"My fight to live"

LISA McCUNE & HUSBAND TIM
on marriage, kids and our new life

OFFICIAL PHOTOS
MARY'S BRAND NEW PRINCESS

THE REAL COST OF LOOKING GOOD
Three beauty budgets

Jamie Oliver's top 10 recipes

IAN THORPE'S NEW PASSION

5 fabulous patterns

THE NO-KIDS DEBATE
Real women speak out

AMAZING PHOTOS
NICOLE KIDMAN

SARAH MURDOCH, RACHEL GRIFFITHS & KERRY ARMSTRONG
unite to save Aussie kids

A few of my favourite things: Covers for the Australian Women's Weekly.

CLOCKWISE FROM TOP LEFT

The beautiful Sarah Murdoch by Hugh Stewart; the divine Nicole Kidman by James White; an ethereal Lisa McCune by Juli Balla.

TOP
*Blessing: Tibetan Gyuto Buddhist monks do a special ceremony for my mother Rae
with my sisters Martha and Sarah, me, Rae and Emma, 2008.*

BOTTOM
My mama and me in Sydney, summer 2009.

'how wonderful'. Even as she lay dying, she thought the idea of Paris 'wonderful'.

Inevitably this got me thinking about the meaning of life, the end of life and my luck in being alive. It made me stop to think about what I wanted to do with rest of my life. I figured I had at least twenty good years to live the way I wanted to, exploring and doing the things I'd always longed to do.

My life-enhancing mother, Rae, was always a great role model for creating an interesting and meaningful life. At a similar age, she was thrown a surprise sixtieth birthday dinner, masterminded by her wonderful close friends, David Marr and Espie Dods. A hundred or so people, film-makers, writers, directors, actors, all of her many friends including some she has had since schooldays, and her family and children celebrated her incredible life and generous spirit. If anybody asks me where my favourite place in the world to eat is, I say simply 'My mother's'. And that was both the joy and the dilemma of my daily life. I began to eat often with my mother. Who can resist a little lamb chop, a fabulous roast chicken and my mother's easy company? I began to wonder if a woman in her fifties should eat so often with her mother. Was I on my way to *Grey Gardens*?

Who was I if I wasn't just the daughter of Rae? Was I just the bossy eldest de Teliga who forced her will on life, the sister to the well-known Sarah (actress and painter) and a swathe of brilliant siblings? If I wasn't the 'successful' media person or the mother of two daughters, who the hell was I? This existential angst was about being alone with myself at last, questioning who I was and what I wanted from life. It was also about being a single, baby boomer woman in the youth-obsessed culture of Australia, getting to the age where you become increasingly invisible. It was a search for new meaning in my life. So I asked myself, 'Okay, so what if you are going to be alone for the rest of your life, how do you want to live? Where do you want to live? What would give you hope for the future? What would give you joy?'

Whoever I was had been submerged a long time ago in the frantic pace of just keeping everything going – juggling a really demanding full-on career while bringing up my children (albeit with the unstinting help of Damien, my very responsible ex-husband). The constant struggle with myself, the questions about who I was and how I wanted to live the rest of my life ran round and round in my brain like a hamster on a wheel.

And so an idea gradually grew in my febrile mind, it grew and groaned, it fluttered and festered, it skipped and it shuddered and it became a plan. I was going to run away from home.

For so long I'd had the feeling that I wanted to live in Europe again. For more than fifteen years, as fashion editor of the *Sydney Morning Herald* and then on *Harper's Bazaar*, I travelled back and forth to cover the ready-to-wear shows in London, Milan and Paris. I got used to the biannual injection of Europe – the beauty, the buildings, the food, the clothes, the shoes and the galleries.

Ever since I was a little girl I had longed to be in Europe. Being part British, part Polish and, truly mixing it up, part Lebanese as well as being fed the myth of European aristocracy from my father, I always imagined I'd live in Europe where I really belonged. I always felt a sense of dislocation from the Australian suburbia I grew up in. I felt like I'd been dropped there by mistake. My father impressed on me the idea of being a Polish aristocrat (fairytale though it may have been), the responsibility of *noblesse oblige* and the duty of behaving in a way befitting such a person. It reinforced my sense of isolation in the hot, baking blandness of the outer suburbs. My foreign name alone singled me out as different.

From the age of thirteen, when I first got pocket money, I began spending it all on international fashion magazines. Inside my head I lived in a European world. From 1964 onwards I pasted pictures, from all the magazines I read, on my bedroom wall. Every few months I created a proto-fashion magazine on my wall – covers of Jean Shrimpton *et al*,

TOP AND CENTRE LEFT
Graduation days for the girls.

TOP AND CENTRE RIGHT
Chez moi.

BOTTOM
Home alone.

fantastic fashion spreads from *Vogue*, *Queen* and *Nova*, and French *Elle* and images of wonderful places I wanted to see. Finally, at twenty-six, I went to Europe, where I lived for two years, learning Italian in Perugia, and then I was awarded a scholarship to study at the British Museum, spending a year in London. I loved living in Europe. Everywhere you turned there was beauty, from incredible buildings to glorious landscapes, from simply delicious food (in Italy, not in 1970s London!), to divinely covetable clothes (I still remember seeing a trench coat lined with rabbit fur, in a window in Perugia and thinking it was the chicest thing I'd ever seen). And after a lifetime of studying art history, there were the incredible galleries, full of works of art that I could see in real life for the first time, rather than in reproduction. And one could never get to the end of it; there was and is always the promise of more. At the risk of sounding precious, the search for beauty has always been my pole star, the navigation point for the way I live my life. I'd always longed to go back and live in Europe, and now there was no reason not to. There was nothing stopping me.

First, I had to ask my girls. One day when the three of us were together, I very tentatively asked, 'I've been a good mummy, can I go now please?' Emily looked alarmed. I explained haltingly that I wanted to live in Europe and that I thought I might live in Paris and – it all tumbled out. Finally Madeleine said, 'Go, Mum, otherwise you'll drive us mad. Just do it.' I had their blessing! Well, more or less. I reasoned that their caring father was in Sydney and so was my mother who they adored, so I wasn't abandoning them, was I?

I set about implementing that plan. I left work, well sort of, with the blessing of my editor-in-chief, Deborah Thomas, who thought running away to Paris was a fine idea. I reduced my workdays at *Australian Women's Weekly* and went freelance. I did as much as I always had but I felt freer.

I put my pretty house up for sale. My sweet little house that I'd decorated with colour – all lavender and pink walls that glowed with warmth and changed tone as the light flooded in. I put in a new bath-room. (Why only then instead of years before?) I cleaned and cleared years of accumulated possessions; I finally let go of all that stuff. I gave away loads of clothes and furniture, threw out the boring accretions from years of living in the same house and pared down to the bare minimum. It sold and I moved into a shabby but great flat that I rented right above my mother (oh yes), in a down-at-heel, liver-coloured brick art deco block, minutes from the beach.

It was cathartic and prepared me well for a life lived with much less. I invested all my money, being told that I would never have to work again . . . yippee! I remember walking down Pitt Street Mall, thinking, 'OMG, I will never have to work again . . . I can do what I like.' So now I had a modest income to live on for the foreseeable future. There it was, all in place, my 'running away from home' money.

I bought a ticket to Europe and packed two suitcases with some clothes (which would mostly prove all wrong for my new life), my techno lifelines – MacBook, iPod and iPhone, my trusty camera, photographs of my girls, a few books, the odd jewel and way too many shoes.

My dear friend Alexandra Joel and her husband Philip Mason threw me a great going-away party with so many lovely friends. It was a wonderful. Now I look back on the photographs and while my friends look adorable, I hardly recognise myself – I looked, well, let's say mature, a bit matronly, a little overweight and a tad 'grand dame' and older than I do now.

Finally, unbelievably, the fateful day came and it was time to GO. I found myself at the airport walking out of my life. And interestingly, like many of the important moments of one's life, there is no photo-graph of my leaving. Just the poignant memory of clutching Emily goodbye (Maddy was in New York) and walking through the airport, overwhelmed by sadness and fear but also elation and anticipation, thinking, 'Oh. My. God. I've done it.'

Yes, I did it. I had finally run away from home.

Farewell Sydney: My party, given by
Alexandra Joel and Philip Mason.

TOP
Alex, Philip and me.

CENTRE
Daughter Emily and Juli Balla.

BOTTOM
Friends Jan Logan, Lee Tulloch
and Jane Roarty.

Flying into the unknown.

CHAPTER TWO

La vie
PARISIENNE

A new country, a new language, a new life

To ease into my new life and allay the massive fear factor, I decided that the best way would be to pretend I was going on holiday, just going on a lovely little holiday and it wasn't really an earth-shattering change of life. I convinced myself that I hadn't just left my entire life behind – my family, my friends my job and my home! I started my 'holiday' by landing in London to stay with my friend, interior stylist Margaret Caselton.

It was one of those magical English summers that beguiles – all dappled green trees and shimmering golden light. Not the grey and drab London of the late 1970s that I remembered from when I last lived there. Even though I had been coming back every year for the last decade to cover the fashion shows, my latest visit made me look at Europe very differently – as home rather than a place to visit for work.

A few weeks later, my two suitcases and I boarded the Eurostar to start my new life in Paris. The Eurostar, the train that rockets under the sea and into France at amazing speed and considerable cost, has become a constant in my life. That first journey, as I sped across the bright green fields of England and France, was so full of anticipation and dreams. It echoed with memories of speeding across the Australian landscape at the age of eight with my grandmother on an ancient sleeper from Sydney to Adelaide, giving me a lifelong love of train travel. In what seemed like a hurtling blink, I arrived in the grimy Gare du Nord in Paris. So began my new life.

Ah Paris! The Paris of all those books I had read and old movies I watched in my teens and twenties. Audrey Hepburn transformed from a brainy, skinny ugly duckling to a gorgeous swan in *Funny Face*. I always imagined that I was that intellectual, very skinny girl transformed by the magic of fashion and the photographer's lens into a vision of Parisian couture-clad elegance. Or in *Sabrina*, the journey of a gangly chauffeur's daughter to chic woman of the world, after her transformative stint in Paris. Or literary heroine, Linda, in Nancy Mitford's *The Pursuit of Love*, one of my all-time favourite books,

First stop London: Summer in Marg Caselton's lovely home.

LEFT *A painter's life in Paris:
My sister Sarah, painting.*

ABOVE RIGHT *Serge Gainsbourg's decorated
tombstone at the Cimitière du Montparnasse.*

BOTTOM *Paris family: Linus, Sarah, Nestor
and Robert Grace.*

who is swept off a railway station and into Parisian life by a dashing French duke.

The reality – I was a fifty-seven year old woman, long past the age of Audrey Hepburn's evocative characters and long past the age to fulfil a magical Parisian transformation as they did. This didn't stop me dreaming then and doesn't stop me dreaming now.

When I first arrived in Paris I went to stay with my painter sister Sarah, her architect husband Robert and their beautiful boys, Linus and Nestor, who lived in bohemian splendour in a wonderful old artist's studio in the 14th arrondissement of Paris, which used to be a space used by artist Alberto Giacometti and his brother Diego in the 1930s.

Entry to this world was through a cobbled courtyard and up some rickety wooden stairs and, hey presto, you felt as if you had arrived on the set of *La Bohème*. Being a classic Parisian artist's studio, one wall is devoted to a cathedral-like expanse of windows flooding light into the apartment overlooking the infamous Montparnasse cemetery. It is here that the many luminaries of French life are buried – simple grey tombstones mark where philosopher Jean Paul Sartre lies beside his lover, the feminist Simone de Beauvoir; the cult singer Serge Gainsbourg is buried, literally, under a riot of souvenirs and mementoes left by ardent fans.

Sarah had lived in Paris since she first moved there with her husband and first baby son nearly twenty years ago. This family connection gave me a mental safety net for my decision to go and live in Paris. Though we could have a somewhat tempestuous relationship at times, she is my much-loved sister. She was *une vraie Parisienne* and it made me feel safer to know she was there.

When I arrived it was summer in Paris and a lot hotter and tougher a city to be in than London. As it gets hotter and hotter Parisians begin to desert the city for their holiday homes. Like lemmings they stream from their workplaces and head south for the summer months. All manner of shops and restaurants begin to close – just as the tourists arrive in droves to enjoy the Paris of their imaginings. Make money, bah! *Pas de tout*! No, it's time for *les vacances* and in true French style they go on as they have always done. You have to admire the French for their absolutely unwavering belief in the superiority of their lives and customs. Even the lure of mammon appears to have no effect on the French. 'Lunchtime, we shut up shop because we have lunch, no matter what. Lunch is a sacred institution. And on Mondays we shut because . . . well, one shuts up shop on Mondays after having shut up shop on all day Sunday and most of Saturday.' (Because France is a traditionally Catholic country there are strong regulations preventing shopkeepers from opening on Sundays, so this strict adherence to customs is even legislated). And, of course, one shuts up shop all summer when the city is teeming with tourists because that is what one does. Resistance is futile if you're living in France so come summer there is no reason to stay in a Paris deserted by the French.

My youngest daughter, Madeleine, arrived in Paris to stay with me at my sister's place while they, as true Parisians, headed on down south, and it was so exciting to see her. It assuaged my longing for my girls, which threatened to derail my newfound freedom. After all it had only been a month or so since I left Sydney. Madeleine is a joy to travel with – easygoing, so funny and with the practical advantage that she speaks French (with a lovely accent after spending a little time in Paris on exchange while she was at school). She is also supremely good-natured; the only time she loses her cool is when I drag her around fashion boutiques. It was clear even at a very early age that Madeleine did not share my 'fashion gene', when she plucked with chubby little toddler fingers at my nude stockings and said, wrinkling up her little face in puzzlement, 'What are dey for? Are dey for keeping the flies off?' The notion that what you wear has a solely utilitarian purpose was already fixed in her brain and it has been so ever since.

Mads and I did all the tourist things I've never had time to do in Paris. We wandered through my favourite places there, particularly the

TOP
Paris: Pantheon and Paris sky.

BOTTOM
*Sister act: Sarah and me
rugged up in Paris.*

ABOVE
*Seeing the sights: Shakespeare and Company
book shop, Paris.*

RIGHT
Mads in the Hall of Mirrors, Versaille.

BELOW
A French rose.

wonderful streets of the Marais, where we visited the magnificent Place des Vosges and the beautiful Picasso Museum. We browsed for ages in the marvellously shabby and evocative English bookstore, Shakespeare and Company. We took one of the *bateaux mouches* down the Seine and stopped off at the Jardin des Plantes and found ourselves in the very quaint 19th-century zoo, with a sloth you could almost touch hanging from a ceiling, complete with a sign asking us not to *déranger* the poor animal. Always loved that French word for 'disturb' with its connotation of derangement.

We marvelled at the roses blooming in the garden of the Rodin Museum, and at the wall of garden planted up the side of the Musée du Quai Branly. We threw ourselves on the grass (not many places you can do this in the manicured confines of Paris) in front of the domed splendour of Les Invalides Museum. We trekked out on the train and waited in long queues to visit Versailles and were rewarded with the miraculous hall of mirrors.

And then I, as a Parisian in training, headed south for the summer. Madeleine, her cousin Linus and I hopped on a TGV, one of the fabulous fast trains of France that make it a dream to travel around. Our train rushed at high speed through France into the magical landscape of Provence with fields of sunflowers, flashes of red poppies in among the green, ochre-tiled roofs and craggy hillsides dotted with pines. Our destination was Nimes, a city as hot as Hades in the summer, but blessed with a history that dates back to the Roman Empire. It is filled with the most magnificent Roman ruins, including the wonderful golden Roman temple in the main square of Nimes, one of the best surviving ancient temples in the world.

Sarah came to meet us and we drove through the villages of Languedoc-Roussillon, an often ignored corner of the south of France, where you can still find yourself in wild landscapes replete with forests and teeming with icy rivers. After years of going south with French friends, my sister and her husband managed to acquire a stone ruin of a house in a tiny village called Esparon, a kind of giant eagle's nest perched atop a mountain in the midst of the Parc National des Cevennes, a UNESCO World Heritage area. The 'stone tent' as my sister calls the house, is cut into the side of the mountain. The bedrooms have whitewashed walls, rough cut into the hillside with unglazed windows that are simple openings in the walls. Known as 'maison troglodyte', the stone houses of the village are traditional centuries-old peasant dwellings carved into the side of the mountain, which are blissfully cool in summer. They are very happy to camp in their stone tent with their bath set in the middle of a stone room and their roofless and almost wall-less kitchen sitting high on the top of the building. When it gets really windy the pots and pans sometimes fly away. The view across the valley more than makes up for any inconvenience in the living arrangements; the view is stupendous and the wind blows the hot air away across the mountains. At night you sit under a peerless moon and dark, dark sky studded with glittering stars – it is magic.

The stone tent, while suitably bohemian for Sarah, is way too rustic for me so she sensibly booked me into the little house across the cobbled laneway from hers. Madeleine and I loved it. With its rooftop terrace that looked across the forested valley, it was sufficiently rustic to be atmospherically charming but blessed with modern plumbing and those prerequisites of an actual roof and walls. Here, I simply ignored the past I had just left and the future that was to come and fell into a blissful present of hot days exploring and walking, then spending cool evenings eating beautiful fresh produce prepared in Sarah's *plein air* kitchen and sleeping soundly with the night wind whispering through the pines.

We climbed up the hill to the white chapel and tiny graveyard amongst the trees above the village. We took long walks through the mountains, my sister looking like something out of a Monet in white Edwardian cotton petticoats, camisole and a battered straw hat. We picked wild figs from flourishing trees, collected bunches of lavender by the roadside, picnicked beside an untamed river rimmed with boulders and swam in freezing, rushing waters. It was idyllic.

All too soon our wonderful summer was over and, as the French do, we made the ritualistic return to Paris for what the French call *la rentrée*. Tired but happy. Madeleine and I caught the TGV back to Paris. My darling Mads went home (oh, so sad) and it was time for me to get 'real' and start the next chapter of my new life.

Sometimes you have to be lucky and my foray into finding an apartment in Paris was one such instance. I'd heard that craigslist was a good place to look (although I know now there is many a scam to trip you up). After searching the ads online I found one for short-term letting called Froggy Flat, which revealed that the French owner had a sense of humour and spoke English. It was in the Marais, very tiny but completely renovated and decorated in simple Ikea modern. When I called, the owner was charming; telling me he and his wife had never done this before and had just renovated the flat. I suggested he consider a six-month lease for a lower rent and he said he'd get back to me. Which he did quite quickly, saying that as his wife was now pregnant it would be easier to let the apartment out for a longer term. Yay! First thing off the list – I had somewhere to live.

The flat was not in the fashionable 4th arrondissement of Le Marais but was in the 3rd arrondissement closer to Place de la République, which turned out to be way hipper. The building was on Rue de Temple, quite a busy road, but it was set back from the street, with windows looking out onto an internal courtyard, making it very peaceful to settle into.

So continued my life lesson in learning to live with less – I had virtually no possessions, no clutter and very little space. It was strangely satisfying. It's really surprising how little you actually need and surprisingly cathartic to live so simply, particularly after living in a full house back in Sydney. The apartment had everything that one could need – a bedroom that could just fit a double bed, a small bathroom complete

TOP *South of France: Sarah, a Monet vision in the woods.*

CENTRE *Still life: Potatoes and Sarah's paintings in the plein air kitchen of their 'stone tent'.*

BOTTOM *Entrance to the bedroom in their traditional maison troglodyte.*

TOP *My return to their mountaintop eyrie in 2013:
Sarah and family with Mama and me.*

BOTTOM *Flaked out in a hammock.*
Photo: Madeleine Hawcroft

with a bath, an even tinier kitchen and a little living room with a convertible sofa. All I needed to buy were some really beautiful French sheets and down pillows and I was set. The flat was small but perfectly formed.

The 19th-century French windows gave me constant pleasure; so lovely in their Parisian proportions. I'd wake up and look at the light filtering so delicately through the sheer curtains and think, 'Heavens, I'm in Paris.' It all seemed to fall perfectly into place, an adorable little *pied à terre* in Paris, a few guide books so I could explore, the local Monoprix where I would do my grocery shopping. What more could one need?

Then the realisation hit me one morning, 'Fuck, I have absolutely nothing to do! I have no one to play with. I am absolutely alone.' After years of living an incredibly demanding life, high-pressure work combined with child-rearing plus a busy social life, it was all gone. The Zen proverb 'Everywhere you go, there you are' seemed particularly apt. I might have escaped my life to go and live in Paris but there I was and I was still me and whatever existential angst troubled me was still there to be dealt with in some way.

The honeymoon was over. There was only me and my motivation, or lack thereof, to spur me on. It was a scary realisation. All those imaginings of how great it would be when I had all the time in the world to laze around, read all the books I wanted, do all the things I longed to do, seemed rather hollow and seemingly without purpose.

The inexorable winter crept up and some mornings I couldn't face going out in that freezing cold or deal with the Parisians; it all seemed too daunting a prospect. Those were the duvet days, when I'd crawl under the covers and not come out. The words, 'Be careful what you wish for' haunted me. Prone as I am to a touch of melancholy (although some of my family might describe it as melodrama), the icy grey days sapped my joy. Even though my sister did live on the other side of Paris, she had a busy family life with Robert and my nephews and she

Paris dreaming: My window in my little apartment in the Marais.

ABOVE LEFT
Paris skyline.

ABOVE RIGHT
Frozen horses in the Jardin du Luxembourg, Paris.

BOTTOM
It's not a dream: Even the graffiti is chic!

was understandably reluctant to take on the role of entertaining me. It was still reassuring to know she was there, though. Family came to the rescue when, in the midst of the freezing winter days, I caught a major bout of the flu and I simply couldn't raise my head off the pillow. Sarah ministered to me, bringing over homemade chicken soup. Thank god for family on this side of the world. It was a real comfort to know I was not going to die in my bed and be found months later chewed by French rats.

If you are going to be melancholy, Paris is the place to do it. Impossibly beautiful, even in the freezing cold, the silvery grey of the sky and the river, the bare tracery of the trees and the golden stone of the buildings merge in a wonderful symphony of tones. After my lowest ebb, sick and home alone, I decided that as soon as I was well it would be time to get out and about. There was no one there to save me but myself. 'You're in Paris, for god's sake. Time to be brave and get out there or you may as well admit defeat and go home.' I took to walking everywhere once I had learnt how to dress for the cold outdoors and the heat indoors – layers . . . always a hat, scarf and gloves and a puffer coat. Taking photographs helped me and gave me a sense of purpose. Capturing the visual beauty around me gave me a sense of meaningful creation. One particularly sad day I walked the quays alongside the Seine, passing the house where Camille Claudel, Rodin's troubled mistress, lived and died. The tragedy of her life made my little bouts of depression seem *très* trivial.

Many Sundays I'd walk across down the streets and across the Seine towards Notre Dame. But that was not my destination; the place I was headed was Saint Julien Le Pauvre, which was built in the 13th century, making it the oldest church in Paris. Years ago I had happened upon it on a Sunday at that time of the sung mass. No grand edifice, St Julien is a simple medieval stone church, but as it is a Melkite Catholic church, it is wonderfully exotic inside, with a sense of deep spiritual calm that comes from centuries of worship. Here at 11 a.m. every

Sunday, the ancient rituals are enacted complete with incense, chiming bells and a small choir of parishioners singing in Greek, French and Arabic. I've been going there for more than a decade and it still fills me with wonder. The elderly man who leads the choir has a sublime voice and when he sings it brings me to tears. I know the faces of the choir and I've seen some of their children grow up over the years yet I have never spoken to anyone. Somehow I've always felt too shy, my French is too poor and maybe in some way it would dispel the mystery of it all.

Afterwards I would spend ages browsing nearby in the atmospheric bookshop Shakespeare and Company. The English language bookshop was started after the war by an American, George Whitman, and has long been a haven for writers and booklovers. Books both old and new line the crumbling walls and spill out onto benches and tables in a wonderfully chaotic way. There is such a sense of literary tradition to discover there. Upstairs, impoverished young students can still bunk down at night on the benches in return for work and they have left poignant little notes of thanks above the benches, full of romantic hopes and dreams of Paris.

And so I began to fall in love with Paris, the real Paris, not just the Paris of my imaginings. And I fell in love with my new life. Slowly coming out of the emptiness of starting from the beginning, I started to put myself back together again. I began, step by step, to refashion my life. I found a yoga studio in rue Saint-Jacques that taught in English, and discovered a style of yoga called Anusara yoga. I rediscovered old friends and made new friends amongst the expats in Paris who lived or worked nearby. People come and go in Paris and burst into your life like shooting stars and then disappear. I discovered that the talented designer/stylist Michelle Jank lived right around the corner from me. Together we went on little explorations of Paris, such as a pilgrimage to the gorgeous macaron heaven, Ladurée, in Place Royale and hung out on the odd glamorous nights at the Ritz and the Plaza Atheneé for drinks.

Divine light: The ancient windows of Saint Julien le Pauvre, Paris.

*Foodie chic: His and hers fruit boxes and the boho delights of the
Marché des Enfants Rouges, one of my favourite eating places.*

Getting to know my local area was a wonderful voyage of discovery. I lived right near one of the great foodie streets, rue de Bretagne – a cornucopia of culinary delights. There was the patisserie with a million little masterpieces in the window and the best baguettes, which people would queue for morning and evening.

My secret squirrel location was the marvellous food market Le Marché des Enfants Rouges, an undercover but still open air market with its little stalls of both fresh produce and little restaurant stalls. It is the oldest covered market in Paris, built in 1615, and the name *Enfant Rouges* refers to 'Market of the Red Children', named after the red coats that the orphans, who lived in the nearby 17th-century orphanage, used to wear.

It became my favourite place to eat. Super Japanese, platters of marvellous Moroccan and a great little 'bio' crepe stand run by a boho Frenchman who quietly mocked the tourists. My sister once heard him say under his breath after an American ordered some peanut butter and jam concoction, 'What are you? Eight years old?' Many a day, in all types of weather, I would sit on rickety chairs at tables in the shabby little market eating delicious food. Often my American friend Mary Gallagher would join me.

Mary's romantic life story is a lovely one. Only a few years before, she had been holidaying in Ravello, a town that sits above the Amalfi coast in Italy, when she noticed a woodcut artist showing his work in one of the little streets of the town. She was captivated by his work and she and her family bought woodcuts from him. A whole year later the family gathered again in Ravello and towards the end of her holiday, Mary found the artist again in a different location. She bought another one of his works and decided to invite the artist to dinner with her family (her Italian had improved since the first time she met him). After dinner, she and the artist, Angelo Aversa, went for a walk in the gardens high above the Mediterranean with a view out to a sea shimmering with moonlight. The rest, as they say, is history. Mary married her

Italian artist and together they had a miracle baby, Cosimo, when she was in her late forties.

Mary was a boon to me during those early days. She had grown up in the American Midwest and had moved to Paris some twenty years before. Mary had worked in fashion for a long time and I had met her years ago when she was doing work for Australian *Marie Claire*. She is blessed with a warm-hearted generosity and a love of hospitality, and I was often around at her lovely apartment in a slightly seedy 10th arrondissement for dinner.

It was at Mary's house that I spent my first Parisian Christmas day, just six months after I landed. It was the first time I'd ever had a Christmas away from my girls and family. It was strange to be without them but it was so different that the hot family Christmas seemed to belong to another time and place. By then I had adapted more to being in Europe and it almost felt like home. There was delight in seeing a traditional European Christmas unfold around me, all twinkling lights in the freezing cold. The excitement of walking at night along the lit-up Champs-Élysées with my sister Sarah and nephew Nestor all rugged up to the nines. A huge decorated pine tree in front of the local *mairie*, Bûche de Noël, the crazy trompe-l'oeil log cakes in the local patisserie, the ice skating rink in front of the Hotel de Ville, Kir royales in Café Charlot with friends. The magic of it almost made up for not being at home with my girls. And I spent Christmas Eve (the important French Christmas feast) with Sarah and her family at home. If I could have had my girls with me it would have been complete.

Friends become so important to a new life when you are away from home. I discovered Australian Maria Vrysakis because friends kept telling me about this marvellous little vintage store in the 3rd arrondissement. At the same time my friend Alexandra from Sydney told me about Maria, who had babysat her daughter Arabella when she was young. Maria had been living in Paris for some years and had bravely opened the store, which happened to be a couple of minutes from my

TOP RIGHT
Friends and family in Paris:
Mary Gallagher and her husband,
artist Angelo Aversa, and son Cosimo
on my first Parisian Christmas.

RIGHT
Hôtel de Ville decked out
in French tricolours.

ABOVE LEFT
Emily with her boyfriend Adrian
and godfather Michael Lynch.

RIGHT
Parisian pomp and circumstance:
A gorgeous Maria in a Martin
Grant dress with her husband
Jean-Francois at their wedding
in Les Invalides.

BELOW
View of the Seine.

apartment. It was a little gem and Maria and I became firm friends, despite an age gap of some decades, and we often sat nattering, having tea and cakes at the counter during the quiet times in the store.

The marvellous thing about no longer working is having time to listen to people's stories and what I've found is that real people's stories are often so much more interesting than fiction. Maria's life story was another wonderfully romantic one. After breaking up with her French boyfriend, Maria, on a whim, went with a friend to the local Fireman's Ball in Paris. These *Bal des Pompiers* take place all over Paris, usually on the night before Bastille day (14 July). Maria and her friend attempted to get into a particular area and was told that it was a VIP area for officers and one was only allowed in if one knew someone. Thinking on her feet, Maria spotted a very handsome French officer, pointed to him and said 'I know him' and was then obliged once she was in to go up and chat to him. *Et encore*, the rest is history. Maria and Jean-Francois Dyoniziak married in the most stunning of location of Les Invalides where officers in the French Army are allowed to marry in the chapel. (Firemen in France are trained as members of the army. They are not only firemen but also paramedics, and are regarded as heroes in France.) My friends Alexandra and Philip and their daughter Arabella came over especially for the wedding and Maria asked me to attend too. It was a once in a lifetime event – a marriage ceremony complete with a fire truck parked in the courtyard and guard of honour of uniformed *Sapeur Pompiers*. The stylish Maria, so tall and elegant, looked divine in a 1930s-style bias-cut silk satin gown designed by Paris-based Australian designer Martin Grant. Afterwards we walked across the green lawns in front of Les Invalides to the Seine where a boat took us down the river to the reception. Maria, her veil blowing in the wind, waved to passers-by in the *bateaux mouches* and it was just wonderful. We disembarked at a small museum dedicated to fairground art and had a fun time whirling around on the fairground rides that still functioned, at this most fabulous of receptions. Now that's what I call a wedding!

While friends, in my case mostly American or Australian, are your sisters in all, revealing the most intimate details of the lives and sharing everything, the French are a different kettle of *poisson*. A very charming French woman, who I have known for quite some time, was telling me about her new boyfriend. However, when I said how much I was looking forward to meeting him she looked horrified and said, without a hint of irony, '*Mais non*, I cannot introduce him to you, you might take him.' That's the competitive nature of the French woman when it comes to men. Given the famed predilection of French men to infidelity, maybe it is simply a wise precaution but it hardly seems very trusting. French women generally don't hang out together in the same informal way and consequently the opportunities to get to know them are limited. In the time I was there I didn't make any new French girlfriends and Paris, despite being the city of romance, yielded nothing in the way of a boyfriend.

However my Aussie expat friends, fashion photographers Chris Jeney and Justin Cooper, along with a new friend, dealer in Aboriginal art Mary Durack, were great to hang out with in the local café for a bit of an aperitif in the evening. Nothing beats that laidback Aussie sense of humour, a perfect antidote to the vicissitudes of French life. One night Mary and I were sitting in Le Progress, a café just near where we lived and I turned to her and said, 'Why on earth do you come here? The waiters are so rude.' She laughed, 'Yes, I know; they are so awful I feel like a battered wife; I keep coming back for more!' At times this was an apt description of living in Paris. The notion of service is somewhat foreign in France; tips are not the norm as the service is automatically included in the bill, so that provides no incentive. But even if it did, visitors to France fail to provide the kind of niceties that French people do as a matter of course. I learnt gradually that failing to say *Bonjour Madame* or *Monsieur* was a grave omission. When I failed to say so to one of the fairly unhelpful staff at the Metro station, the woman at the counter castigated me and said to me in French, 'The English never say *bonjour.*' From that day on, even though saying it seemed forced, I tried to say *bonjour* before I said anything else. Then you are required to follow up with a courtly ritual of politeness to flatter, wheedle or cajole to get whatever it is you want.

But the main problem was my appalling French – it simply was not good enough. Why did I imagine that with my rusty schoolgirl French I was suddenly going to burst into fluency? I sounded like a crazed three-year-old toddler when I was speaking French or worse, an uneducated barbarian. One French silver fox said to me that I would never be taken seriously in Paris because my French was so bad. That's when I resolved to take formal lessons. Learning French in Paris is a frightening experience, as David Sedaris' hilarious account in his book *Me Talk Pretty One Day* attests. I snorted out loud after reading that his teacher said she would rather have a Caesarean than teach him French.

There was nothing particularly amusing about going to the Alliance Francaise – the bureaucracy alone was scary. They make you sit a test to mark your level of competency. Pathetic was the only description of my endeavours. The whole tenor of education in France is based on critical analysis. In Italy if you say 'mozzarella' or 'spaghetti' with just a hint of flair, the Italians exclaim how well you speak Italian while in France, a pursed lip, a sharp rebuke or complete incomprehension are the more likely outcomes of attempting to speak the language.

And even when one has mastered the basics, it is the weird familiarity of certain words that trip up even the more seasoned French speakers. My sister Sarah recounts visiting the rather smart butchery on the Ile Saint Louis and asking for *jambon sans preservatif*. What she thought she was saying was 'ham without preservatives'; what she actually said was 'ham without condoms'. On a subsequent visit, she was trying to ask the butcher could she cook the meat in a pan; what she actually said rather than *a poele* was *a poil*, a colloquial term for 'naked'. The butcher answered, quick as a flash, '*Comme vous voulez, Madame,*' (translated into 'as you wish, Madame'). She is sure she could hear the

whole shop guffawing as she slunk out of the butcher shop clutching her parcel.

While my French continued to be fairly poor, I had one big advantage that overcame that lack. After years in fashion I knew how to dress and dress well. It's a language that the French speak fluently. Once I discovered early on that my velour tracksuit pants, although *de riguer* for my weekends in Sydney, were not acceptable in Paris despite being designed by Sonia Rykiel, I wised up about what is important to the French. I divined this after searching a smart department store to find such attire relegated to the far-flung corners of the sports section. As far as the French are concerned tracksuits and joggers were for sports, nothing else. I love Australian Sarah Turnbull's story in *Almost French* about being chided by her French husband for nipping out in her tracksuit pants to the *boulangerie* because 'It's not very nice for the baker'!

And in what other country would the following happen at Immigration. Picture this: I'm in the Eurostar terminal and a rather cute French immigration officer rushes up to me. Good grief, I thought, what have I done wrong . . . are they going to arrest me? 'Madame, I think thees is ze belt for your trench coat!' he said, pushing the belt into my hands. Where else on earth would you find a male officer who would care about a trench coat belt, let alone work out who it belonged to and make the effort to return it to you because he knew it was important?

Clothes maketh the man or woman in France. When I decided I needed a French bank account I attempted to open one, only to be met with stony faces and lots of *non, non, pas possible*. I decided on a plan of action that involved wearing a lot of expensive cream cashmere. I did my hair and make-up, donned said cashmere and sundry discreet pieces of jewellery, then entered the bank. Lo and behold an appointment to see the manager was immediately forthcoming. At my appointment I shamelessly flashed an article I had written for London's *Financial Times*, which I had been commissioned to write by their fashion editor Vanessa Friedman, about how living in Paris had changed the way I dressed. It was by me, about me and it had a lovely picture of me by French photographer Magali Courouge sitting in Café Charlot, my local, in . . . cream cashmere. The combination was a winner; a bank account was immediately arranged. However, I was well and truly hoisted on my petard because he gave me the most expensive premier account, which I have unsuccessfully attempted to shed ever since, paying most of my meagre funds in fees.

Paris is the place of legend in fashion. For a young girl growing up in the suburbs of Sydney, spending all her pocket money on international fashion magazines, Paris was the dream, the apotheosis of all things fashion. Coming to live here was the fulfilment of that dream and a limited budget was no deterrent from trawling the designer stores of Paris. After all this is place where fashion began; where Worth began the tradition of haute couture at the end of the 19th century, where Coco Chanel invented a new modern way of dressing, where Christian Dior saved French couture with his post-war New Look and where Yves Saint Laurent shocked the establishment with his ready-to-wear line, Rive Gauche, and fabulous tuxedo dressing.

Top of the must-visit list is always the great French houses: the classy grey and white charm of Christian Dior in Avenue Montaigne, the fabulous Hermes store in rue Faubourg Saint Honoré and the original rue Cambon boutique of Chanel. I never tire of such a fashion pilgrimage and when my friend Alexandra comes to Paris we have a glorious day trawling Avenue Montaigne and rue Faubourg Saint Honoré, just as excited as if it were our first time.

For the best fashion floors in Paris, Le Bon Marche department store, over on the Left Bank, has the 'it' brands of the world all in one place and the added bonus of a fantastic food hall, where I shopped often for food arranged in country sections. A somewhat extravagant yet wonderful way to do your grocery shopping!

For fab French beauty brands, groceries, inexpensive fashion and

Style

All wrapped up in Paris

Moving from Australia to France, **Jane de Teliga** finds a change of wardrobe is not just a matter of keeping warm

In one of the most crazily romantic gestures of my life, last summer I sold my palm tree-shaded cottage 10 minutes from the ocean in Sydney, left my job as style director of Australia's biggest magazine, the Australian Women's Weekly, kissed my daughters, mother, sister and friends goodbye, and moved to Paris. Instead of having a hot bright sunshiney Christmas, I find myself under the cold wintry skies of Paris, in a bijou (very small) apartment in the Marais.

My work as mother was done, my daughters finished university and off living their lives. I was in burnout mode after eight years in a demanding job, and it was possibly the last time I could embark on such a life-change. So off I went, alone and in my 50s, to an uncertain future, my only work being as European fashion correspondent for Australia's national newspaper, the Australian.

Mostly it's been wonderful, sometimes it's been hard. There was a lot I wasn't prepared for, beginning with day to day communication in my bad schoolgirl French with the butcher, baker and candlestick maker. But what has most surprised me as autumn has faded into winter is that my move from southern to northern hemisphere involves not just a change of lifestyle but also a change of wardrobe – and that this sartorial switcheroo isn't solely about the weather, but cultural value systems themselves.

I left behind a youth-obsessed culture focused on a beach-ready body beautiful (i.e. Elle Macpherson), with which I was increasingly at odds, and landed in the country where women of a certain age such as Anouk Aimée, Jeanne Moreau, Catherine Deneuve and Fanny Ardant were actually celebrated. Here it isn't so much about the body beautiful as beautiful clothes to cover that body.

Even though there is a winter in Sydney, for example, generally Sydneysiders live in denial. I did have a winter coat – a black cashmere overcoat, used when I covered the collections – but mostly it sat in the spare wardrobe, mild-ewing. I once wore the coat to a meeting in Sydney to be greeted by a Frenchman with the words "Jane you look like you have come off ze Russian front."

Now I have three coats, all military-styled, all shades of the Russian front,

Vive la France: It's perfectly acceptable to be grown up in Paris, says Jane de Teliga
Magali Corouge/documentography

and I wouldn't think of going outside without one: either the Tara Jarmon double-breasted, belted, black wool trench that pulls in tight against the icy winds, or the See by Chloé cream felted wool greatcoat, or Martin Grant's double-breasted, dove-grey, swing jacket. In them, I feel like a grown-up in a place where it is perfectly acceptable to be a grown-up.

Walking the beautiful monochromatic streets around my local quartier or strolling over the Seine from a yoga class near Notre Dame, I notice there isn't a Frenchwoman who doesn't have some sort of scarf arrangement knotted around her neck, and I understand that what I had once seen as a fashion victim's accessory can have a real purpose: wrapped, looped, tied or worn babushka-style around my head, the scarf becomes my closest ally. And hats, used only in Sydney for the races or the beach, are no longer an affectation but a necessity.

All this is made ever more immedi-ate since, along with my old life, I also left my four-wheel-drive car behind when I moved. In Sydney I motored everywhere (just before I left Australia I attempted a train ride with one daughter, who felt it necessary to instruct me on how to insert my ticket in the machine); now metro tickets and Oyster cards litter my handbags and pockets, and I am learning to dress for public transport. Early on in my adventure my youngest daughter came to visit and stated emphatically

on a metro ride that I "looked too rich". I laughed (salary was one of the victims of my move), but dutifully, if generally unsuccessfully. I have been attempting a slightly grungy Charlotte Gainsbourg/Kate Moss look. I tell myself nobody need know that my flat, rubber-soled boots are actually snakeskin Miu Miu and cost a month's rent.

Now, in my tiny apartment my high heels sit abandoned in the cupboard like a litter of unwanted kittens; my white linens, kaftans and cottons lie in limp piles like old tea towels next to my Balenciaga doctor's bag, whose lack of a shoulder strap almost resulted in a frost-bitten hand. I have become a convert to the non-obvious It bag slung across the body, in the form

Here it isn't so much about the body beautiful as beautiful clothes to cover that body

of a black Longchamp flat nylon style and a new Miu Miu with both hand and shoulder straps.

And yet, through all the adjustments, I feel a strange sense of being European that I had even growing up in Australia with my funny, foreign surname, my English grandmother, Slavic grandfather and father born in Poland. It seems to radiate out from the cellular level, in a way that was never apparent in the brilliant sunlight and heat waves of home. I wear my coats, scarves, hats and boots and feel like I belong.

Here I am in Paris, it's Christmastime, it's freezing, I am all dressed up and anything is possible.

TOP
My article for the Financial Times, *London about my life in Paris.*
Photo: Magali Corouge.

LEFT
Hôtel Plaza Athénée in Paris.

bits and pieces for my home, there is the fabulous supermarket Mono-prix near Republique where I used to live. And you'll find branches all over Paris. I bought homewares such as pretty Yves Delorme sheets and blankets from the department store BHV just near Hôtel de Ville (the building that houses the City of Paris administration). This department store has an amazing hardware floor in the basement that draws *les gens* like a magpie to sparkle.

Even while I lived in the 3rd arrondissement the rapid march of gentrification began to change the streetscape and little boutiques began to spring up like wildflowers in the tiny streets. Often as fast as they appeared, they disappeared when the global financial crisis began to bite. One longstanding habitué of the 3rd is Australian designer Martin Grant and I love visiting his studio/store in rue Charlot to drool over his tailored couture-like creations.

For chic designer labels (in the mid-price range), *les Français* have really got the market sewn up with stores for chic contemporary labels like APC, Isabel Marant, Vanessa Bruno, Sandro and Maje. My favourite shopping street in all of Paris was and still is the rue Vielle du Temple that begins right up in the 3rd near rue de Bretagne and heads down towards the Seine with a profusion of cool shops, bars and eating places. When my eldest daughter Emily and her boyfriend Adrian came to Paris for a week in the New Year while I was living in Paris we happily trawled from Vielle du Temple in the 3rd through the Marais in the 4$^{th.}$ Emily, unlike her sister, has inherited the fashion gene and it was wonderful to have her in Paris doing the boutiques together and eating in the famous Jewish quarter around rue des Rosiers. Because the Marais has been historically the Jewish area of Paris, this is one of the few places where most shops are allowed to open on Sunday. So the Marais is the place to be on Sunday and is teeming with people promenading along rue des Francs Bourgeois, hanging out in cafes and darting in and out of the boutiques along the way. The street takes you on a journey from ancient to modern Paris as it runs from the beautiful historic Place des Vosges right along to the Centre Georges Pompidou, the contemporary art museum, famous for its exposed ducting and colour pipes, which has a stunning view of Paris from the rooftop.

Another popular pastime in the shopping stakes in Paris are the flea markets. The whole idea of flea market shopping sounds appealing but really there is nothing 'flea market' about the prices. The enormous Marché de Clignancourt is an entire village with streets and a labyrinth of shops so complex that I leave it to the experts, my friends Pam Easton and Lydia Pearson of the divine Brisbane label, Easton Pearson. They have been coming to Paris for years for their showings during the *prêt-à-porter* and they are the ideal guides, showing me the best boutiques for vintage clothes and textiles. Could I ever find them again? Not a hope in hell. I found the Vanves flea market much more manageable and affordable – it's just a few down-at-heel streets filled with lots of ratty little treasures. There I found my much-loved little mother of pearl Buddha that I wear round my neck every day. He is the happy Buddha of abundance and when I'm feeling poor I rub his round pearly tummy for luck.

To be able to visit the world's most beautiful museums and some of the greatest art exhibitions after years of studying art history at school and then university was such a buzz. I have to admit that until I lived in Paris, the only time I went to the Louvre was to see the fashion shows. At the Musée d'Orsay, all the Impressionist and Post-impressionist works I studied in art history are still surprising in their brilliance and vivid freshness, from Gauguin's primitivism filled with raw sensuality to Van Gogh's luminous colour that vibrates with life. If you search you might find, tucked away, the still shocking and scandalous image in art history by Gustave Courbet called *L'Origine du monde* ('The Origin of the World') of a woman's most private parts. My mother once famously said to someone, 'Well, I've seen the c—t picture.' My mama may be in her eighties but she still loves to shock.

ABOVE *Seen in Paris: red rose in restaurant at the top of the Pompidou centre.*

LEFT *Christmas Fiat at the marvellous 'merci' store.*

BELOW *Emily and me in the Palais Royal.*
Photo: Adrian Deutsch

TOP LEFT *Adorable stone lion in front of Saint Suplice.*

TOP RIGHT *Scenic Paris: The Louvre from the banks of the Seine.*

BOTTOM *Me in the midst of the Musée d'Orsay.*
Photo: Emily Hawcroft

My other favourite museum is the beautiful Picasso Museum, not far from my favourite street, rue Vielle du Temple. The museum building alone is worth the visit, not to mention the collection deeded by the complicated Picasso family in lieu of inheritance tax. And then there are all the wonderful temporary fashion exhibitions in Musée des Arts Decoratifs, part of the Louvre on the rue de Rivoli, with an outdoor café on the Jardin des Tuileries that is perfect for a sunny day *déjeuner*. At the Jeu de Paume on the end of the Tuileries are not-to-be-missed photography exhibitions from the great photographers of the world, as well as the spectacular special exhibitions held at the Grand Palais (I saw some amazing fashion exhibitions there including Yves Saint Laurent and Valentino). At the post-modernist temple of the Pompidou Centre, not only can you see wonderful contemporary art, it doubles as vantage point for the best views across Paris. From there, spread out before you are the great landmarks of Paris from the Arc de Triomphe to the church Sacré Coeur high on the hill. And to help you navigate your way around this fabled city I've listed some of my favourite places on the following pages (60–65).

GETTING AROUND A CITY

———

Catching public transport taught me where everything was in a new city, and walking everywhere made me much fitter. No car meant no maintenance costs, no insurance and no petrol, which is astronomical in Europe. Much to my children's amazement I learnt to catch public transport in Paris and London, whilst at home in Sydney they feel it necessary to instruct me on how to put my ticket into the slot at the train station turnstile.

The Tube in London and the Metro in Paris are absolutely the best ways of getting around and are way cheaper, quicker and easier than driving or catching a cab. First thing to do in London is buy an Oyster card; for a small refundable deposit you get a plastic card that you can top up easily, which works out so much cheaper than buying individual tickets. The Tube in London is a modern miracle, even though the locals gripe about it, and the Tube staff are endlessly helpful with directions.

Buy a carnet of tickets in Paris and you can pop out anywhere from the metro and find what you are looking for. Just steel yourself for the ever-present smell of urine, and unlike London, don't expect much advice or assistance from the staff. Get a Metro plan and just do it.

✳

THE LISTING
PLACES I LOVE TO SHOP IN PARIS

———

APC

www.apc.fr
112 rue Vielle du Temple
75003 Paris, France
Telephone: +33 (0)1 42 78 18 02

This store sells cool neo-preppy clothes for the young, but I can often find a cute piece here and there that suits me.

Le Bon Marché Rive Gauche

www.lebonmarche.com
24 rue de Sevres
75007 Paris, France
Telephone: +33 (0)1 44 39 80 00

My favourite department store in Paris, where I go to see all the best French and international labels, drool over the wonderful shoe selection, and also pick up delicacies at the Grand Epicerie, a magnificent food hall.

Colette

www.colette.fr
213 rue Saint-Honoré
75001 Paris, France
Telephone: +33 (0)1 55 35 33 90

The cult store for the super-fashionable with great music, cool trinkets and the best curated international labels.

Didier Ludot

www.didierludot.fr
24 Galerie Montpensier – Jardin du Palais Royal
75001 Paris, France
Telephone +33 (0)1 42 96 06 56

The legendary vintage designer store with scary prices to match, but marvellous for a browse amongst beautiful couture garments and Hermes bags, as is the wonderfully spare Palais Royal itself.

L'Habilleur

44 rue du Poitou
75003 Paris, France
Telephone: +33 (0)1 48 87 77 12

Discount designer wear for both sexes from Paul & Joe and other brands. Good knitwear can be found at excellent prices.

Isabel Marant

www.isabelmarant.tm.fr
47 rue de Saintonge
75003 Paris, France
Telephone: +33 (0)1 42 78 19 24

A *très* cool store by this Parisian designer in the hip streets of the 3rd arrondissement. Jane Birkin shops at the rue Jacob store. One time I was browsing there when I heard someone call 'Jane', turned to answer and realised it was Jane Birkin they were calling.

Isabelle Subra Woolworth

51 rue de Seine
75006 Paris, France
Telephone: +33 (0)1 43 54 57 65

A tiny store filled with brilliant antique jewellery. I go there to feast my eyes and dream.

Les Lunettes d'Also

www.leslunettesdalso.com
115 rue Vielle du Temple
75003 Paris, France
Telephone: +33 (0)1 48 04 93 52

For super-cool eyeglasses. I love their frames.

Marché Biologique de Boulevard Raspail

Boulevarde Raspail (between rue de Cherche Midi and rue de Rennes)
75006 Paris, France

Act like a Parisian and visit the fabulous food market on the Boulevarde Raspail. This is the place my sister and her husband shop weekly for food. It has a wonderful organic market every Sunday.

Marché aux Puces de Clignacourt, also known as St Ouen

Association Des Puces De Paris St Ouen
142 Rue Des Rosiers
93400 Saint-Ouen
Telephone: +33 (0)1 40 12 32 58

Where to begin – the famous flea market covers the area of a large village with about 3000 stalls. It requires stamina and recommendations. My friend Alexandra buys vintage Chanel jewellery from Olwen Forest. Marche Serpette, Alle 3 Stands 5 and 7, rue des Rosiers St-Ouen, while the Easton Pearson girls love finding vintage textile swatches and clothing in the stalls all over the market.

Marché aux Puces de Vanves

www.pucesdevanves.typepad.com
Avenue Marc Sangnier and avenue Georges Lafenestre.
750014 Paris, France

A slightly down-at-heel market on a more manageable scale with stalls for furniture, jewellery and vintage clothing, plus an even rattier section strewn across the pavement.

Martin Grant

www.martingrantparis.com
10 rue Charlot
75003 Paris, France
Telephone: +33 (0)1 42 71 39 49

I adore Martin's neo classic couture-tyle tailoring and you can get a peek into his showroom, which also serves as a boutique. Devoted clients include Lee Radziwill (Jackie Onassis's sister), and Sarah de Teliga (my sister!), who has known him since his Melbourne days.

Merci

www.merci-merci.com
111 Boulevard Beaumarchais
75003 Paris, France
Telephone: +33 (0)1 42 77 00 33

This is a kind of mini department store and a shopping experience with a philanthropic purpose. I love browsing here as I know that the profits go to charity.

SHINE

www.shineparis.com
15 rue de Poitou
73003 Paris, France
Telephone: +33 (0)1 48 05 80 10

An international multi-label store
for the 'It' girls of Paris.

VANESSA BRUNO

www.vanessabruno.com
100 rue Vielle du Temple
73003 Paris, France
Telephone: +33 (0)1 42 77 19 41

The chic Parisian label for the
modern girl. Lou Doillon (Jane Birkin's
daughter) and Kate Bosworth are
her poster girls.

PLACES I LOVE TO EAT

———

L'AVANT COMPTOIR

9 carrefour de l'Odeon,
75006 Paris, France
Telephone: +33 (0)8 26 10 10 87

A crazy crowded French 'tapas' bar
with basically a counter and a series
of intriguing bite-sized morsels. A lot
of fun, I went with my nephews, who
adore it. Next to le Comptoir de Relais,
the proper seated brasserie and on the
other side a great little crepe place.

CAFÉ CHARLOT

www.cafecharlotparis.com
38 rue de Bretagne
75003 Paris, France

On the corner of rue de Bretagne and
rue Charlot, it's open for breakfast,
lunch and dinner and is a mecca for the
cool set of the third. My favourite café
when I lived around the corner and still
my favourite for steak *hachee* and *frites*,
the French hamburger and chips.

LE CHATEAUBRIAND

www.lechateaubriand.net
129 avenue Parmentier
75011 Paris, France
Telephone: +33 (0)1 43 57 45 95

The new French food in a very hip,
spare restaurant, whose food seems to
polarise opinion; my sister took me for
my birthday and we loved it. Super cool
and listed as one of world's top places
to eat. Try it if you are experimental
and can stand the queuing.

CHEZ NENESSE

17 rue de Saintonge
75003 Paris, France
Telephone: +33 (0)1 42 78 46 49

'You do realise,' said my friend Maggie
Alderson, 'that we have slipped into the
forties,' when I took her to this old-
fashioned family restaurant.

Hotel Le Meurice

www.lemeurice.com
228 rue de Rivoli
75001 Paris, France
Telephone: +33 (0)1 44 58 10 10

My favourite high-style bar with the evening sky ceiling in Paris, which is filled with fashion editors during the *prêt-à-porter*, a meeting place for designers like Alber Elbaz, and in recent years a show venue for Collette Dinnigan. For Alexandra's birthday we had a fabulous dinner in 'Le Dali', the Philippe Starck-refurbished lobby restaurant where we were looked after superbly. Grand but lovely with an even grander gilded salon restaurant next door.

Ladurée

www.laduree.fr
Ladurée 16 Royale
16 rue Royale
75008 Paris, France
Telephone: +33 (0)1 42 60 21 79

The divine painted room is just the place to indulge in their famous macarons in deliciously pretty colours. For me it's always their sublime sundae, *Coupe Plaisirs*, with vanilla and raspberry ice-cream, fresh raspberries and cream. Truly decadent.

Marché des Enfants Rouges

39 rue de Bretagne
75003 Paris, France

The oldest covered market in Paris, with a fab array of eat-in stalls from Moroccan to Japanese. You can eat at the rickety little tables in all weathers.

La Perle

78 rue Vieille du Temple
75003 Paris, France
Telephone: +33 (0)1 42 72 69 93

The bar for the cool Parisians, it is infamous as the bar where John Galliano insulted fellow drinkers and as a result lost his job at Dior.

Rose Bakery

30 rue Debelleyme
75003 Paris, France
Telephone: +33 (0)1 49 96 54 01

Created by an English woman named Rose Carrarini. It is full of the kind of healthy food that it is hard to find in Paris. Delicious housemade quiches and great cakes.

PLACES I LOVE TO STAY

———

For places to stay in the Marais, check out this handy website listing hotels from 4-star to budget: www.parismarais.com and sign up for their newsletter. My Marais picks would be the beautiful Le Pavillon de la Reine and Hotel Bourg Tibourg.

HOTEL BOURG TIBOURG

www.bourgtibourg.com
19 rue Bourg-Tibourg
75004 Paris, France
Telephone: +33 (0)1 42 78 47 39

A jewel-like hotel with rooms as tiny as the word 'bijou' suggests, right in the heart of the Marais.

LE PAVILLON DE LA REINE

www.pavillon-de-la-reine.com
28 Place Des Vosges
75003 Paris
Telephone: +33 (0)1 40 29 19 19

This charming ivy-clad hotel right on the glorious Place des Vosges has been a favourite for many years of the Easton Pearson girls. Now refurbished, it's pricy but splendid.

PLACES I LOVE TO GO

———

LES ARTS DECORATIFS

www.lesartsdecoratifs.fr
107 rue de Rivoli
75001 Paris, France
Telephone: +33 (0)1 44 55 57 50

Just along from the Louvre, the museum of decorative arts shows many exciting fashion exhibitions, and has a wonderful shop and café where you can eat al fresco in the Tuileries.

ÉGLISE SAINT JULIEN LE PAUVRE

www.sjlpmelkites.fr
1 rue Saint-Julien le Pauvre
75005 Paris, France
Telephone: +33 (0)1 43 54 52 16

Known as the oldest church in Paris, it is a beautiful contemplative space with a wonderful Sunday sung mass by the church's choir.

Jeu de Paume

www.jeudepaume.org
1 place de la Concorde
75008 Paris, France
Telephone: +33 (0)1 47 03 12 50

Fantastic photographic exhibitions are held here. I've seen amazing Diane Arbus and Richard Avedon shows.

Musée d'Orsay

www.musee-orsay.fr
1 rue de la Légion d'Honneur,
75007 Paris, France
Telephone: +33 (0)1 40 49 48 14

An incredible museum that shows Impressionist and post-Impressionist works in a grand 19th-century railway station refashioned as a gallery.

Musée National Picasso

www.musee-picasso.fr
5 rue de Thorigny
75003 Paris, France
Telephone: +33 (0)1 42 71 25 21

The magnificent 17th-century building houses a huge collection of Picasso's work.

Shakespeare and Company bookshop

www.shakespeareandcompany.com
37 rue de la Bûcherie
75005 Paris, France
Telephone: + 33 (0)1 43 25 40 93

Atmospheric and adorable English language bookshop, still the same after more than six decades.

WH Smith

www.whsmith.fr
248 rue de Rivoli
75001 Paris, France
Telephone: +33 (0)1 44 77 88 99

The huge English bookshop just near the Place de La Concorde has a massive selection of international magazines and many interesting author events.

ABOVE
A drift of roses: John Rocha's poetic design for spring/summer 2014 at London Fashion Week.

RIGHT
Mirrored catwalk at the Acne show at London Fashion Week.

CHAPTER THREE

A fashionista IS BORN

LONDON, ENGLAND

My lifelong love affair with fashion

Why fashion? Why this lifelong passion for fashion? I cannot really explain it in any logical way. Was it at age four, dressing in a little gold velvet dress and ballet slippers as a flower girl for my aunt's wedding? Or was it the beautiful fine panama straw hat, trimmed with pale pink silk flowers, bought for me by my grandmother Kath when I was five in a smart hat salon in Rowe Street, Sydney? Who can say what sparked my fascination? Who was this skinny little girl with the long plaits who lay in bed at night and wished so hard for a pair of red shoes to appear at the end of her bed in the morning? And the yearning teenager in the late sixties who created a bedroom wall covered with fashion images cut from international magazines?

All through my teenage years I longed for beautiful clothes. I had my mother running up things from McCall's patterns chosen from the pattern books that I pored over in David Jones where we bought very expensive Italian silks, which we made into an empire-line red gown for my first dance or a hot-pink and red full-length shift when I imaged myself after an Italian Contessa I had seen in *Vogue*. My mother acted as my dressmaker and while she always looked smart, my total obsession with fashion was not inherited; I appear to have been born with it. Born with an innate longing for beauty that has possessed me since childhood. I remember one big date with my first proper boyfriend, David, who had asked me to the regatta. A big deal for a nice little private schoolgirl. I travelled into town to pick up my new pantsuit from Merivale, caught the train back to change and then the train out to the regatta and arrived, super-groovy, in a lime-green pantsuit with white shirt and yellow chenille tie, just as the last race was finishing. I had missed the entire event, such was my dedication to fashion.

For me fashion has always been an aesthetic experience, literally a way to fashion my life. As women we are so lucky to be able to create ourselves every morning. It is the self-creating aesthetic that has absorbed my attention all my life. Even though I got hived off the fashion trajectory into a university degree, where I studied Fine Arts

LEFT *Couture by Christian Lacroix*
BELOW *John Rocha: Romance in 2013 at London Fashion Week.*

*Extraordinary creations
for Christian Dior,
designed by John Galliano.
Shown during the
Paris couture shows 2008.*

and Italian, I always adored fashion. It was unthinkable in my family that one would want to work on a fashion magazine. When I won a Commonwealth scholarship it was assumed by all, including myself, that I would go to university. Later, after a year in London on a scholarship to the British Museum, I scored the job of a lifetime when I became a curatorial assistant at The Art Gallery of New South Wales, and on the arrival of the adventurous Edmund Capon I managed to marry my fascination with fashion to art when he gave me the opportunity to do a small project show called *Art Clothes*. The exhibition captured the blossoming of fantastically creative young Australian designers and artists working at the time, such as Jenny Kee and Linda Jackson, and a whole colourful explosion of interest in Australiana. The show created so much interest and became the springboard for many other exhibitions that I created and curated such as *Art Knits* for the Bicentennial, which travelled the regions of New South Wales and then went on to Japan and Korea, and *Australian Fashion: The Contemporary Art*, which showed at the Powerhouse Museum and then in London at the Victoria and Albert Museum, where it proved very popular with its explosive colour and print to London audiences. Finally, it was bringing the *Christian Dior: The Magic of Fashion* to the Powerhouse Museum that changed my life unexpectedly.

It was the Dior exhibition that I negotiated to bring to Sydney from Paris that turned my life full circle, back to my obsession with fashion, when the visionary newspaperman John Alexander, who was also a trustee of the Powerhouse Museum, asked me if I would be interested in being the fashion editor of the *Sydney Morning Herald*. 'What do you think we should be doing?' he asked me one day at lunch.

'Well,' I said, 'if you really want to be a world-class newspaper, the *Sydney Morning Herald* should be reporting on the international shows, using top fashion photographers to shoot fashion stories for the pages . . .'

'When do you want to start?' he said and in one fell swoop my life changed and I made the switch from museum curator to fashion journalist. I was suddenly the style and fashion editor (I chose my own title) of the *Sydney Morning Herald* and I was diving into the deep end as soon as I hit the newspaper offices. There was no special attention and nobody to tell me how to do my job. It was sink or swim and it was tough proving myself under the baleful eye of much more experienced writers. While I had written a few pieces over the years and many introductions to catalogues, I had never actually been a real journalist.

From the beginning of my journalistic career I was in a powerful position within the fashion industry; a position of enormous privilege and influence. I decided, right from the beginning, on becoming fashion editor that I would use that influence in the fashion world for good, to really support and showcase the great talent that was developing in Australia. I always aimed to praise beauty and genius from the world of fashion and encourage new Australian talent, and to create the best fashion images with great fashion photographers. I never felt any desire to gossip or bitch or waste precious column inches on the bad, mean or ugly.

There was always the thrill of discovering an emerging designer like Akira Isogawa, giving him the award for best new designer, in a dreamy outfit we devised together of layers of beautiful sorbet-coloured georgette, which I subsequently gave to the Powerhouse Museum for its collection. Or the first time I went to see the newly discovered designers from Brisbane, Pam Easton and Lydia Pearson, in a tiny serviced apartment with the marvellous Jane Roarty, who has the best fashion eye in Australia. Many of the outfits I bought from them over the years, I also gave to the Powerhouse's collection.

For five full-on years I was both the stylist and the writer, producing fashion shoots and a fashion column weekly for the pages of the *Good Living* section, plus writing for the news pages of the paper. Into the gaping maw of the newspaper I poured my images and words. Today these kinds of jobs are usually done by more than one person, such as

LEFT
*Pam Easton and Lydia Pearson
at the Louvre in 2008.*

BELOW LEFT
*Akira Isogawa in Paris
showing his creations in 2008.*

BELOW RIGHT
*At a Collette Dinnigan lunch
at the Hôtel de Crillon with
fellow fashion journalists
Melissa Hoyer and
Maggie Alderson.*

Ethereal creation by Antonio Berardi at London Fashion Week 2013.

freelance stylists and writers and a fashion editor on staff. The pressure I felt was immense at times but was relieved a little by the appointment of shoot assistants – first up, the perky Sam Griffin and then quirky and creative Nicole Morgan. Towards the end of my stay at the *Herald*, the brilliant writer and now my good friend Maggie Alderson arrived on *Good Living* and she wrote on all things food- and style-related and we would share the fashion writing. Producing a new fashion shoot virtually every week for fifty-two weeks of the year was exhausting but so exhilarating. Creating a concept and sourcing all the clothes, choosing models, make-up artists and photographers; it was like producing a mini magazine every week. For me it was a dream come true. My teenage years of putting magazine pages on my walls was finally realised in real life. And I got to work with some of Australia's best fashion photographers. My god, I worked so hard then and looking back on that heady time in my life I don't know how I survived. Let alone my poor children, who had a single mother working full time plus going out to events in the evening! Someone once told me there were three key people one had to have at a fashion event and I was one of them. The pressure was constant. Thank god for a supportive ex-husband and an exceptionally kind friend, Lynn Watson, who embraced my children into her family fold of five girls every day after school. I will be eternally grateful for that incredible support. That is the real secret as to how I survived the work/life juggle.

From that brief conversation over lunch in 1994 began a decade of me going to and reporting on the international ready-to-wear collections. My first trip to Milan resulted in the first fashion story ever on the front pages of the *Herald* in its 160 years. The story was about Isabella Rossellini appearing on the catwalk of the Dolce & Gabbana show in Milan and my next front-page fashion image was of Elle Macpherson in the Thierry Mugler show in Paris. While we now take it for granted that fashion stories appear around the world on the front pages of newspapers, at the time it was a radical move by the inspired John Alexander, who cleverly saw the future of newspapers. At the time many of the male journalists were outraged that fashion could be taken seriously enough to appear on the front page and somehow didn't see the innate sexism of their reaction. Fashion was considered a lightweight subject in the journalism hierarchy, traditionally relegated to the special women's section at the back of a newspaper on a particular day. Sport, however, was considered a vital subject that appeared ad nauseam alongside a constant stream of political intrigue everywhere and every day. That was in the olden days and now fashion is a major component of reporting in newspapers all over the world whether fashion news, editorial fashion shoots or reports on the shows.

While I was at the *Herald*, twice a year I would trek off to Europe to the frontline of fashion, leaving behind my domestic life and two small children with my ex-husband for the incredible *stürm und drang* of London, Milan and Paris in full fashion swing. So began all the fabulousness and all the torture of the shows. What people imagine as incredibly glamorous, air-kissing, fluffy bunny kind of stuff was, in fact, incredibly exhausting work – going to hundreds of shows, filing copy almost every night until the wee small hours, slogging through the metros and streets at all hours. You can always tell the difference between magazine girls and newspaper girls. The international mag girls hang around in their exclusive posse, look incredibly glamorous, always have bare legs no matter what the weather (never, ever wearing naff hosiery), and have drivers and cars that they spend hours searching for and phoning up on their mobile phones, 'Giovanni,' they wail, 'where are you? We can't see you!' and proceed to sulk because they have to walk a block in their stilettos on their stick-thin bare legs. Newspaper girls, however, travel solo, often look frazzled and exhausted, dress to keep warm and comfortable so they can survive in all climates from freezing cold to heat-wave conditions and cope with all manner of public transport. Newspaper girls, who have been up all night filing copy, are pathetically grateful on the rare occasions that someone, one of the grand fashion mag girls, actually offers them a lift.

I can remember tortured nights in Milan, when the internet first became available, running downstairs in a dressing-gown to the hotel office at three in the morning, desperate to file copy for the next day. In those early days the internet connection was clunky and unreliable so I would resort to filing the copy over the phone, word by word, spelling out V E R S A C E to some hapless woman who had never experienced fashion-speak before. One memorable result was trying to use the word 'genteel' and it ended up being filed as 'gentile' (probably in my exhaustion I said the Italian word 'gentile' meaning polite or kind), so we ended up with gentile [sic] hemlines. *Media Watch* made great fun of this; even the *Jewish Times* had a good laugh referring to 'gentile' and 'non-gentile' hemlines!

I was right there in the infancy of Australian Fashion Week when Simon Lock met with me and the chic Nancy Pilcher, editor of *Vogue Australia*, for the first time to tell us with his characteristic bravado about his grand plans for Australian fashion. He wanted to create a proper fashion week to rival the *Prêt-à-Porter* in Paris that would put Australia on the international fashion map. We, along with hard-working journalist Melissa Hoyer, encouraged his big idea. Lock, with his particular blend of charisma, vision, bullshit and sheer determination made it happen and it grew into the full-on Australian Fashion Week he always envisioned.

My dogged push to profile fashion in a modern and significant way was something that didn't always endear me to the hardened news journalists, particularly after the brilliant and somewhat Machiavellian John Alexander left the *Sydney Morning Herald*. The editors that came after him generally had the idea that fashion reporting was doing a dreary business story on the demise of an Aussie swimwear label. A joyless non-visual negative male take on fashion that had little to do with the passionate desire of women to be able to access beautiful, amazing fashion imagery and inspiration.

Reporting on fashion weeks, no matter where in the world they happened, was both exhausting and exhilarating. Around day three, I still fall into a slump, which I call Fashion Week Syndrome, when I get depressed and want to escape the indignity of it all. In Australia it was much easier as the smaller pool meant that I was among a group of major movers and shakers in the fashion food chain. Everybody knew who you were, so you were looked after and cosseted with automatic seating in the front row. Internationally it was and still is a lot tougher, a reality check or what I came to call my Buddhist lesson in humility. Queuing in the freezing cold, being shoved around in the crowd, turned away by fifteen-year-old PRs, wandering lost and alone in some godforsaken place, suffering blistered feet, lack of food and sleep, being refused tickets to sought-after shows, staying up half the night writing copy – the list goes on. But then there are the highs – the incredibly beautiful collections, the sheer genius of the creators' imaginations and their amazing show visions, the chic on the streets, the amazing parties and general fabulousness and heady buzz that gets into your blood. Fashion shows are so much like childbirth in that you forget the pain, remember the highs and by the time the next season comes around you are raring to go again.

There were some incredible shows in those years that still linger in my mind. In London the rawest and most amazing of all were those of Alexander McQueen – from his early show in 1997 held amongst burning braziers in Borough Market (no health and safety then!) then moving to a traditional catwalk show spiced up with the shock of incredible flaming fire bursts or thunderous rain showers (the one time you did not want to be sitting in the front row). The most beautiful shows I have ever seen were McQueen's savagely poetic and extraordinarily beautiful shows held in a disused London bus terminal. In the cavernous space whole imaginative worlds emerged from the darkness and for the brief half hour or so we were transported into other worlds of dark, lyrical beauty. I think of the show set in a winter wonderland

*Telephone-box red:
My British colour of choice
at London Fashion Week
in 2011 and 2013.*

*Photo (bottom):
Dominic Farlam*

full of snow and trees where the snow-covered catwalk space turned into an ice-skating rink, with some of the models suddenly skating across the ice; or the show where huge robots spray-painted the dress worn by Shalom Harlow; or the incredibly poetic insane asylum show in 2001 where models in glorious feathered dresses stalked the padded walls of a glass-sided room.

In Paris the vignettes that flash into my mind from the *Prêt-à-Porter* are the incredible romantic theatricality of John Galliano's shows for Christian Dior – all fabulous sets, extraordinary play-acting and exaggerated makeup, the *belle époque* extravagance and multi-patterned mash-ups of Christian Lacroix's artistic vision; or chatting backstage after Stella McCartney's show to her immensely proud dad, the charming Paul McCartney, who tried his best Aussie accent on me.

In Milan it was the panache of Tom Ford's sexy reworking of Gucci – just one smile from Tom backstage and I was in love; he has that effect on people, both male and female. Also the incredible glamour of Gianni Versace's supermodel goddesses clad in figure-hugging gowns – Christy Turlington (for me the most beautiful woman in the world), Naomi Campbell, Kate Moss and the supermodels of the time, and the ultimate Italianate sexiness of Dolce & Gabbana or the celebrity-studded front rows and mind-boggling parties of Giorgio Armani.

The very first time I ever went to the shows was in Milan. It was just at the time when Italian fashion was usurping Paris as the creative fashion epicentre. Italy and Milan were uncharted territory and at this point no Australian journalists had ventured into this Milanese fashion wonderland. I was booked into what turned out to be a budget hotel – maybe brothel – near the main railway station. I had heard that the Hotel Principe was the fashion hotel; however, I was booked into the wrong Principe, with absolutely nothing princely about it. I was shocked by the arrival of an amorous Italian at my door in the middle of the night. Clearly this was nothing unusual for this particular hotel and they simply showed him up to my room. The next season I moved hotels. One freezing day I was so jetlagged and exhausted by the shows that I took to my bed. When I woke up the city was white and hushed and I looked out to see that it had snowed while I was sleeping and the strange fascist façade of the Milan railway station was covered in pillowy frosting. The grime had turned into magical beauty and I felt like I was on the set of Bertolucci's incredibly evocative film set in the thirties, *Il Conformista*.

My first few fashion shows in Milan were eye-openers – and that wasn't just the runways. Naively I thought that being a fashion editor, I could simply rock up to the shows I wanted to see and they would let me in. I soon found out that I had to beg for tickets. The only thing in my favour was that they thought that the *Sydney Morning Herald* was somehow related to the *International Herald Tribune*, where the legendary Suzy Menkes reigned as the hard-working, most respected newspaper fashion editor in the world. I remember fronting up at the Giorgio Armani show and grudgingly being given a ticket to watch the catwalk show standing up behind the back row. The very next season, when they were planning to open an Armani store in Sydney, I was suddenly catapulted into the front row, just a seat away from Sophia Loren, and was also asked to a small private dinner at Giorgio's apartment. Such were the highs and lows of fashion week from the sadly seedy to the incredibly glamorous, from the sublime to the ridic-ulous. I was in agony as to what to wear to that dinner and remember frantically cobbling together a black evening outfit and later climbing the majestic stone stairs leading up to Armani's apartment in his centuries-old palazzo, feeling a little like the country mouse. In Armani's world, all cream and parchment and sleek modernist furni-ture, I sat completely overwhelmed on the immense cream sofa, eating pasta with white truffle grated over the top and with a wide-eyed stare watched as the likes of Eric Clapton and Martin Scorsese walked past me. This first-time panic melted a little after a season; I began

TOP LEFT *The romance of the rose from John Rocha 2013.* TOP RIGHT *Florals by Mary Katranzou.* ABOVE LEFT *Fashionistas at London Fashion Week, 2013.* RIGHT *The chic Charlotte Dellal, designer of the cult shoe label Charlotte Olympia.*

I'M SO VERY BOURGEOIS

RUNNING AWAY
FROM HOME

83

ABOVE
*(from left) Olivia Palermo at
a London Fashion Week show,
Freida Pinto and Dita von Teese
backstage at Burberry, London 2012.*

feeling like an old hand and attending them no longer fazed me. At one of Armani's big parties a very tall and tucked Faye Dunaway glided by while the delightful Fiona Macpherson, then editor of British *Harper's Bazaar* admitted to me how overwhelmed she felt being there. It made me realise that I was not the only one who felt a bit out of her depth.

Working in the media gives you amazing access to a world of wonder, but you really need to guard against being too caught up in it. Such is the ridiculously fickle nature of fashion and the international shows that if you get notions of your self-worth and ego tangled up in the hierarchy and politics of it all, it can really do your head in. Your seating allocation does not equal your worth in the world! Nor does hanging around at swanky fashion parties equal real life. It can be mind-bogglingly fabulous, it can be really fun, but it can also be isolating and unnerving too. But in the end it's like taking part in some ridiculously lavish stage play or theatrical game. Somehow one needs to hold on to one's own centre, and core spiritual values, while all around you some crazy alternative universe careens off into la-la land.

For a few months every year I got to lead a jetsetting life of glamour. It was like being a kid and playing a wonderful game in the world of the rich and famous. But I always reminded myself to keep my head. One season Autore Pearls asked if I would like to borrow some South Sea pearls to wear to the collections in London, Milan and Paris. I only had time to pick them up on the way to the airport and was gob-smacked by this incredible strand of perfect, lustrous pearls the size of ping-pong balls, valued at a couple of hundred thousand dollars. I was so terrified of losing them that I wore them all the time, even on the plane. I arrived in London wearing a black David Jones tracksuit and the pearls, only to discover that my luggage had somehow disappeared. So for the first few days of London Fashion Week I wore the DJ's tracksuit covered by my dear friend Craig Markham's very chic Paul Smith trench coat with the priceless pearls and nobody seemed to think this was at all unusual. At a fabulous dinner at Dolce & Gabbana's glamorous Milan home on a hot Milanese night, I wore the pearls again. They were so big no one thought they were real until one international journalist who had been to Australia to write a story about South Sea pearls said, 'Oh my god, those are real!' I was very happy to return those most beautiful mill-stones around my neck when I got home.

When John Alexander left the *Sydney Morning Herald*, he was snapped up by Kerry Packer to run Australian Consolidated Press magazines. Not long after, Alexander said to me, 'I have something for you but you need to keep an open mind.' I wondered what it could be. But when it was announced that the glamorous Deborah Thomas was to edit the publishing icon, *The Australian Women's Weekly*, I had an inkling of what was to come. Before long I was ensconced at the *Australian Women's Weekly* in a newly devised job as style and fashion director, to work on revamping and recreating the images that appeared in the magazine. It was a really exciting chance to modernise an Australian legend that had been the most popular magazine in Australia since the 1930s, read by one in four women in the country. At the same time a role was created for me on *Harper's Bazaar* with the title of fashion features editor-at-large so I could continue to cover the international fashion shows. Once upon a time *The Australian Women's Weekly* gave Australian women their news on the Paris fashion shows but the media universe in Australia has long since expanded to include the world's top fashion titles like *Vogue* and *Harper's Bazaar* and that's where the truly fashion obsessed now go for their news.

My job as style and fashion director at the *Weekly* was elephan-tine so after a few years of juggling, my focus became solely *Australian Women's Weekly*. As much as I tried I couldn't do both jobs. However, I really missed the high drama and sheer inspiration of going to the international shows.

The longing for all that drama and beauty never leaves you once you have been bitten by the fashion show bug. When it became known that I was flying the Sydney coop and moving to Paris, Georgina Safe,

*In the pink: Designs by the inventive and always surprising Christopher Kane,
London Fashion Week 2012.*

then of *The Australian* newspaper, asked me if I wanted to be European fashion correspondent for the paper. It was a no-brainer – living in Paris and reporting on fashion again! I remember, at the time, talking to Nicole Kidman while we were shooting the Nintendo campaign and her saying to me, 'Of course you must do it!' Not often you get encouragement from an Oscar-winning actress! I agreed and was really excited to get back in the fashion show saddle. September 2007, when I moved into my little apartment in Paris, was also the month I returned to the shows. And the shows were a lot easier this time around as I knew so many media people from around the world who attended them, as well as the PR people who controlled who got tickets to what. Basically I was a lot less in awe of the whole process and a lot more experienced. Starting with London Fashion Week was a buzz. Just as before there was the fizzing anticipation of seeing something new and wonderful. I've always loved London shows for that reason – they are so adventurous and unpredictable and my first return season was no disappointment. Thinking I'd never see any one as exciting as Alexander McQueen again, suddenly on the catwalk there are the designs of young Glaswegian Christopher Kane and I'm backstage in a flash interviewing the twenty-five-year-old as he talked about being inspired by the crocodile-wrestling Aussie Steve Irwin. Go figure. I was just one of a few that day backstage but these days you cannot glimpse the top of his head through the throngs surrounding him after each show.

After London it was on to Milan for a glamour fix. This was the place it all began for me and I used to love going there to see the architecture and taste the food, and for the window-shopping. Now it's Donatella Versace's pared-down take on her brother's legacy of glitz and glamour, ten years after his murder. For some things, the more they change the more they remain the same and it was a joy to see again the unpredictable and prophetic weirdness of Miuccia Prada, where I saw Lara Stone for the first time, in a strange fairytale Arthur Rackham-inspired show. Now one of the world's biggest supermodels,

Lara Stone was pretty unknown back then and she walked around the meandering Prada runway in a fairytale-illustrated skirt; the fashion pack was fascinated to see real bosoms under a strange knitted vest. Much discussion ensued post-show about her large and clearly natural breasts, a sight so unfamiliar on the catwalk, where the norm is preternaturally skinny girls. Hallelujah, a curvy girl on the catwalk!

Paris is always a glorious opportunity to see beautiful shows and that season on my return it was back to John Galliano for Christian Dior looking a little like a reprise of his greatest shows without the same excitement. Paris is also the place to see the Australians on the world stage. The two Australians on the official calendar were Collette Dinnigan and her pretty shows of girly lace gowns at the beautiful Le Meurice Hotel, and Paris-based Martin Grant and his couture-inspired tailoring shown in the wonderful setting of the chapel at École des Beaux-Arts. Going with my sister Sarah and her family to Martin's shows is always a special experience, and this particular show was set in the extraordinary surrounds full of enormous plaster casts of famous sculptures. My nephew Linus was studying architecture here, which made the event particularly wonderful. Putting your family and the shows together is an especially heart-warming experience, even though it was below freezing and the fountains in the courtyard had frozen solid.

Other Australians present their collections in fabulous showrooms in Paris and it's great to see those talents that I loved and nurtured in the early days of my fashion journalism career showing their designs in the most important fashion city in the world, where buyers throng not just to go to the catwalk shows but also to stalk the myriad show-rooms to buy the work of many other international designers. Akira Isogawa shows in the splendidly artistic surrounds of Philippe Model's 18th-century apartments painted in a rainbow of colours. To visit my dear friends Pam Easton and Lydia Pearson of Easton Pearson in their showroom in the beautiful Le Pavillon de la Reine Hotel in the Place

Paris-based Australian designer Martin Grant's
show in the Ecole des Beaux Arts, Paris.
Cobalt blue and neon pink later featured
in his designs for the QANTAS uniforms.

TOP *Preen's take on 50s couture crossed with 70s punk at London Fashion Week.*
BOTTOM *A fab marabou confection by Brit milliner Stephen Jones.*

des Vosges, the most glorious square in Paris, is a treat. The tail end of the '*Prêt*' in Paris is often the treasured few days I get to hang out with the Easton Pearson girls, who always know the best places to eat and shop in Paris (see chapter 2 for inspiration).

After years of doing the ready-to-wear designer shows in Paris it was the chance to 'do the couture' in January 2008 that really let me live the dreams of my teenage years. Haute couture (literally 'high sewing') by its very nature is the pinnacle of dress as an art form. Couture, the cauldron of ideas often dubbed the laboratory of fashion, is created for the privileged few who can afford to spend hundreds of thousands of dollars on a gown. Yet the couture creations are extraordinary art for art sake's pieces that are enjoyed by the many as they are instantly disseminated by print, video and Internet around the world. People have been predicting the demise of couture for decades but mercifully it somehow survives with a handful of designers showing their couture collections twice a year only in Paris. After years of breathing in the heady atmosphere of couture via magazines all those years ago in the 1960s when it was at its zenith, I finally got the chance to go before it all passes into history.

For me the apotheosis of couture was the Christian Dior show I saw that season, held in a Napoleonic tent in the Bois de Boulogne, where the showmanship and genius of John Galliano shone in a way it used to. Inspired by the *belle époque* art heroines of Gustave Klimt and the like, the Dior show was a dazzling theatrical confection of extravagant gowns, extraordinary hats by Stephen Jones and ridiculously wonderful hair and make-up. For the first time I took my own photos to capture the show and so began my ongoing learning curve with digital photography to record what I saw at the shows. I felt like I was capturing a little bit of history, in a way that's probably what it was, considering the self-destructive demise of Galliano at Dior more recently.

And to go full circle on the Armani experience of my first days in

Milan I got to go to Giorgio Armani's couture show in Paris. At the very glam Armani Privé in the art deco splendour of the Trocadero, Giorgio Armani's foray into the rarefied realm of couture, I did something I had never done before – I asked a legend to pose with me for a photograph and thrust my camera into a friend's hands. In that split second I thought I should do something about an icon passing by and knowing I had a camera handy . . . Hey wait a minute why not get a photograph with the legendary star? The result is here: the extraordinary Sophia Loren in her full glory, looking Amazonian and magnificent with a little shrinky me standing beside her like some overawed schoolgirl. As I get older I realise that life is lived moment by moment and one has to grab those moments before they pass by forever. *Carpe diem* is a sadly overused phrase but as I age it becomes more and more apt.

While in Paris I went to some fabulous events as the European fashion correspondent for *The Australian*. I was invited to Rome to attend a major Bulgari celebration. What a sumptuous few days it was in the eternal city bathed in golden light, including a beautiful candlelit dinner in an aristocratic palazzo filled with old masters and a once in a lifetime visit to the Bulgari workshop to watch millions of euros worth of precious stones being painstakingly set into dazzling necklaces. The legendary jewellers were part of the 1960s Roman jetsetting scene of Elizabeth Taylor and Richard Burton during the heady days of the making of the movie, *Cleopatra*. On that visit I was able to sample a little bit of that 1960s jetset magic and live that life for a few days. This trip was so very different from my first trip to Rome in my twenties, staying in some flea-bitten hotel and ending up in an ancient ruin of a hospital with vicious food poisoning.

Another special event I covered for *The Australian* while I was living in London (more about that later) was a sumptuous Paris-Londres Chanel collection: the brilliant Karl Lagerfeld brought his annual Métiers d'Art show for the first time to London. My friend Claudia Crow, who I had met through London Fashion Week when she was the

LEFT *Fab fashionista Anna dello Russo at London Fashion Week.*

ABOVE RIGHT *With Manolo Blahnik after an interview I did with him for* The Daily, *London Fashion Week's newspaper.*

BOTTOM *The stupendous Sophia Loren dwarfs me at the Armani Privè show during Paris Couture 2008.*

TOP *Giant jacket for the Chanel couture show in 2008.*

BOTTOM LEFT *The famous mirrored staircase in the Chanel store in Rue Cambon, Paris where Coco Chanel used to sit and watch her parades.*

BOTTOM RIGHT *Karl Lagerfeld at the special one-off Chanel show in London 2007 with model Yasmin le Bon.*

very dynamic PR consultant for the British Fashion Council, invited me to this particular event and what a dazzling show it was, not only for the beautiful collection but also for the audience. It showcased the incredible artisanal work of the small historic Parisian ateliers (such as Lesage, the wondrous embroiderers) that create the detailed work of couture and have been saved by being bought by the house of Chanel.

I hung around after the show so I could take photographs (my newfound interest) and get some quotes for my piece for *The Australian*. I got the chance to chat to one of my favourite actresses, Emma Thompson, who was as friendly and unpretentious as I had imagined she would be. Her scene in *Love Actually* where she realises her husband is having an affair is a *tour de force* that is etched on my brain. Clad in an all-white androgynous, latter-day Annie Hall outfit complete with running shoes, she was incongruously bejewelled in Chanel diamonds. 'I'm a fashion show virgin,' she exclaimed, having never been to such a show before. I also chatted to the extraordinary contemporary fashion icon Daphne Guinness, who said when I asked her what she was wearing: 'All Chanel couture. Is that sad?' 'Nice work if you can get it' is what came to mind! Most fascinating was watching Kaiser Karl himself in all his white-ponytailed neo-Edwardian splendour at the after-party, beguiling the guests and switching seamlessly from one language to the next. I realised he had his own elderly waiter who followed him everywhere around the party as his personal butler, holding a silver tray bearing a single glass of Diet Coke. When people ask me if what you see in fashion films like Robert Altman's *Prêt-à-Porter* or *The Devil Wears Prada* is pure fantasy I have to reply it's way more fantastical and weirder than you could possibly imagine.

For me the excitement at the shows is not just about what is worn *on* the catwalks but also what is worn *off* them. Watching the fashion crowd from around the world is the most powerful source of fashion information one can have, as Tommy Ton's brilliant images seen on Style.com, of the show-going fashionistas attest. It is watching the international fashion editors and what they are wearing that really reveals what is going on in fashion. It is the real catwalk. As I age though I notice how easy it is to become invisible in this fashion world after a certain age. The new fashion bloggers and street photographers began to annoy me in that they would photograph anybody outlandishly clad in a bit of torn neon tulle and ratty old vintage as long as they were young, while ignoring the beautifully dressed older women no matter what they were wearing or who they were. Deciding to redress the imbalance I started my London blog, 'What the grownups are wearing' on my styleoncall.co.uk website, showing exactly those women. I plucked up the courage to ask some of the older luminaries in the fashion world if I could photograph them and record what they were wearing and they loved the idea. But I'm not that brave about it so I asked those I knew, including myself (I couldn't say no and I figured if I am going to ask this of others I have to be prepared to do it myself. Live by the sword, die by the sword!). Some of those I plucked up the courage to photograph include Lee Radziwill, Lucinda Chambers, Sally Singer, Sarah Mower, Franca Sozzani and Anna Wintour (but at a distance as I don't fancy being pushed aside ignominiously by the bodyguard she travels with). In a few years the interest in older stylish women has grown exponentially with the growth of many style blogs, the return of many supermodels to advertising campaigns and editorial, with an interest in septuagenarian, octogenarian and beyond style. Dressing stylishly as you get older is much more difficult and those who do it well really stand out.

I feel incredibly lucky to be a part of the fashion media both in Australia and internationally. All in all it's been an incredible privilege to be allowed access to these events and shows and it attests to the power of childhood visualisation. The beautiful clothes and the amazing ingenuity of the designers who come up with new visions each season continue to inspire me each season. Just when you think you're bored with the whole damn thing, someone creates something

ABOVE
*Anna Wintour, in her signature blunt bob
and shades, at the Burberry show in
London 2011.*

RIGHT
*Me at the entrance to the show, held in
a vast tent in Kensington Gardens.*

LEFT
*Paloma Faith backstage
at the Ashish show, 2013.*

BELOW
*Me and my designer hero Alber Elbaz of Lanvin,
at the International Woolmark Prize judging,
London 2012.*

so breathtaking and ingenious that you are caught up again in the glittering web of fashion. Inside, I am still the child who lay in bed at night and wished for red shoes to appear by magic. That childlike sense of wonder and longing still captures me when I see the shows. Sometimes at night, instead of counting sheep, I imagine what I would wear if I could afford anything in the world. To quote Daphne Guinness, 'Is that sad?' Let me see – some quirky Prada pieces, something delicious for evening from Valentino, an incredible baroque embroidered dress by Dolce & Gabbana, super-sharp menswear tailoring from Celine, magical fitted suiting from Alexander McQueen, a fabulous evening coat and jewels to match from Lanvin, a matt-black crocodile Birkin from Hermes. The never-ending possibilities of dreaming.

And dream I still do. I'm still covering the shows in London, long after I thought it would be over for me in this world. I'm even writing for *The Daily*, *London Fashion Week*'s own newspaper. Nowadays my writing can take the form of anything from a traditional printed piece to an Internet gallery with extended captions. The media has changed dramatically and rather than harking back to the good ol' days, I have learnt to adapt and diversify – and I'm enjoying the trip. 'Going with the flow' is definitely my mantra. I've embraced the new media with my own blog and I've done fashion reports for Wool.com and media feeds for the Woolmark Facebook page. My friend Lisa is hugely entertained about the time I spent recently as the social media editor for Woolmark – 'Only you could be a social media editor in your sixties!'.

I caught a glimpse of some of the legends of the fashion world deciding which young designer to award the Woolmark prize to in 2012, reviving the heady days of the International Woolmark Prize when the top prizes went to Yves Saint Laurent and Karl Lagerfeld in 1954.

It was especially exciting as I got to spend time with the endearing Alber Elbaz, the much-loved designer for Lanvin and one of my fashion heroes. I've been seeing his shows since the very beginning of his career and he always impresses me with the sweet and savvy things he says about the relationship between love, passion, fashion and women.

For me fashion has and always will intrigue me. Fashion reveals the world around us by conjuring up our fantasies and desires in dress form. It dreams fantastical dreams and tells stories about what is happening and how we are thinking. It can be a thing of profound beauty or extreme ugliness. It can be, by turns, crassly vulgar or sublimely beautiful and it still holds me in its thrall to this day.

TAKING PHOTOGRAPHS AND HAVING MY PHOTOGRAPH TAKEN

Aside from one course on travel photography I know little about photography and even less about cameras but what I do know I've learnt through trial and error. That's the great thing about digital cameras: you can point, shoot and discard at no cost. I am hopeless at the technical stuff so experimenting is the only way I learn. And I'm still learning. One thing I learnt from Michael Potter when I went on the travel photography course is to not walk around with your camera in the camera bag; you need to have it to ready to use immediately. This seems obvious but it makes a big difference to how many shots you come back with.

I've discovered that, as well as the big scenic shots, little details can really evoke a place. Framing and cropping in on a picture can make it seem fresher and more alive. And don't be shy to ask to take a shot of someone, as people are usually flattered if you ask to take their photo.

After years of shooting fashion with photographers I know that harsh sunlight is never good, so earlier in the morning and later in the afternoon is better for photographs and shooting people in shade often gives better images.

Want to get a good photograph taken of yourself? Stand at a slight three-quarter angle (it's more slimming), shift your weight to one foot to create a shapely curve, pull your torso up (imagine the string at the top of your head), pull your tummy back towards your navel, turn your face towards the camera and find the light with your face and give a big smile. Let go of the self-talk ('I always take a bad shot') and just do it. Take a minute to put on a bit of lippie or move to better light (not full midday sun as you'll squint) or background so you don't waste a shot. My friends tease me about styling a shot but if you want a good one that's sometimes what you have got to do. Looking away and then looking back at the camera makes for a fresher, more genuine shot.

✳

London life: My flower-themed flat in Belsize Village.

CHAPTER FOUR

London CALLING

Another city, another fresh start

Once you have made one momentous change, you can go on to make other similarly big changes because the fear factor is no longer there. You figure you've survived and prospered since the last big change, so why not? When my fabulous former assistant, the divinely named Clementine O'Hara, told me she had seen a job going for a fashion director in London on *Good Housekeeping*, the much-read British version of the American women's magazine, I thought why not? I was ready to get back to work. One imagines longingly, when you are working really hard, of a life lolling about reading, eating, sleeping and travelling but the reality is that after a while it all seems a bit purposeless and self-indulgent. And even a bit lonely if you are on your own. In Paris there was always a sense of being just an observer, an outsider to the life going on around me. I knew I would never really be part of Paris life; the language and cultural mores set me apart. Paris is a transient city for many expats, with friends often coming and going. I loved London, had lived there before and have had friends there for years. I knew I could slip into life there so easily. I knew I could be happy, really happy. By now I felt the desire to be creative and work in magazines again. My depleted energy and ideas had been well and truly restored in Paris. I missed the camaraderie of working with colleagues, the feeling of doing things in a team, of creating images together. I longed to get back to being a real part of life and real work. I believe that life presents opportunities when you are ready for them and you just have to be open enough to receive what the universe presents to you. That is how I've learnt to live my life in my latter years, something I wish I'd learnt sooner.

So I contacted the newly appointed editor Louise Chunn at *Good Housekeeping*, who I had met briefly the year before in London and we talked over the phone about the job. I was delighted to find she was enthusiastic to meet up again. She's a straight-talking New Zealander, despite many years in London, so we understood each other and had a similar down-to-earth sense of humour. I felt I could work with

Rule Britannia (CLOCKWISE FROM TOP): *Scots Guard; dual phone boxes in Primrose Hill; St Paul's cathedral.*

Colour wash (CLOCKWISE FROM TOP):
Violet door in Hampstead; pastel terraces in Notting Hill;
rainbow viewed from my Maida Vale apartment.

her. I knew *Good Housekeeping* was a British publishing staple along the lines of *The Australian Women's Weekly* (although surprisingly with a much smaller circulation considering the size of the population). With a major frump factor, *Good Housekeeping* was ripe for a style make-over and I always love a challenge. Louise popped over to Paris one day for a meeting over lunch. I felt the occasion demanded something very Parisian and a bit grand so I chose Le Grand Véfour, a magnifi-cent-looking restaurant where Napoleon often supped with Josephine. Set in the incredibly elegant Palais-Royal, one of those classical formal squares that make Paris so beautiful, Le Grand Véfour opened in the late 18th century and is tucked away at the end of the Palais Royal arcade, all neo-classical gilt and red velvet banquettes. It is truly a place with a sense of occasion and just the place to make a life-changing decision.

All went swimmingly and Louise and I agreed on a time to start in March, just a few months away, so I gradually took my leave of Paris. At the shows in Milan in February I remember turning to Vanessa Friedman, the formidably clever *Financial Times* fashion editor, saying, 'I'm moving to London in three weeks and I have nowhere to live!'. In her super-efficient way she forwarded an email there and then from a PR she knew who was letting out her studio apartment in Holland Park. I looked at the photos of the quirky but charming-looking abode, googled the location (I thought it looked lovely but it turns out that a street or two in London can make all the difference) and took it sight unseen.

The fact was, yes, it was in the rather grand Holland Park just minutes away from Clarendon and Portland Roads and lovely Elgin Crescent but it was actually right smack-dab in the middle of a council housing estate, right above a rather grimy convenience store. My friend, artist Loene Furler, was once staying with me and popped downstairs for a pint of milk and overheard two local women comparing notes about their respective sons' prison sentences. Just half a minute away people are driving around in Bentleys and living in £4 million houses painted in candyfloss colours. Is it because of my middle-class Sydney sensibilities, where rich and poor live in separate enclaves, that this seems very strange to me? The egalitarian part of me sees the logic in exposing the rich and poor to each other but the other part wonders if this is just too cruel an exposure for those without money to have their noses rubbed in such wealth.

I have never felt poor before but living in London makes you feel that way. Now I am more inured to the stark contrast of rich and poor but when I first came to live in Holland Park it shocked me – both extremes – the obscene wealth and the stranglehold of poverty and class. In Sydney we are used to living in our comfortable middle-class enclaves, yet in London there has long been a policy of mixing rich and poor together, with council housing in the midst of grand streets. London is so much more affluent than ever before as the European, Russian and Middle Eastern rich pour money into the streets, houses and stores. Many ordinary London families can no longer afford to live there and are moving out into the towns and village outside.

I was so excited to be coming back to London and was bursting with such a sense of anticipation and a feeling of joy. Not a moment's regret about quitting Paris, which I knew was just a Eurostar trip away and not a twenty-four-hour-long haul. There'll always be Paris and as Piaf sang in 'Je ne regrette rien' – the moment I landed in London off the Eurostar, I knew I was home.

It was the Easter weekend and spring had sprung spectacularly in the streets around Holland Park with extraordinary fluffy pink blossom bursting from the trees. It was so pretty that I was in heaven and went about obsessively photographing the drifts of pink blossom. The apartment itself was quaintly adorable; a big bohemian studio with a separate kitchen and bathroom and I felt really excited to be living in London again after forty years. I lived my dream in Paris and I'm so glad I did, but as the old adage I keep coming back to says, 'Be careful what you wish for because it might come true.' It did and I did it and that was

A fashion shot I styled in Morocco.
Photo: Graham Shearer

Loving markets: Portobello Road market chandelier
(TOP); *Marylebone farmer's market* (BOTTOM).

enough. Before long on that very first weekend, the weather suddenly turned freezing and I watched in wonder as flurries of snow swirled outside my windows covering the fluffy pink blossom with fluffy white snow. It was magical. I sat alone in my shabby little flat and felt so joyful to be there.

Oh, the ease of speaking your own language! Ask a question at the tube station and some helpful guy tells you what you need to know, so unlike Paris where finding someone to help is impossible. When the dreadlocked West Indian dude behind the counter at Holland Park tube station said, 'Sure, darling, tell me what you want,' I was close to tears with gratitude. 'I've just come from living in Paris,' I croaked. 'You are sooo kind.'

I adored the area around Holland Park and Notting Hill, if not the immediate vicinity of my apartment. I completely fell in love with Portobello Road, just a short walk from my place. Despite the fact that on Saturday it's crawling with tourists and so crammed you can barely move, I just loved the whole energy. Getting off the street into the Portobello galleries and pottering through the ramshackle stalls manned by ageing eccentrics is just such a buzz. From silverware to old lace, paintings to china, the centuries seem to tumble out before you, throwing mementoes of bygone lives in your path. I went into nesting mode buying old cutlery and plates and had a big splurge on the most beautiful old Moldavian rug woven with oversized cabbage roses, which is the central motif of my decorating, along with a patchwork quilt made by my mother. And just nearby are the chic boutiques of Westbourne Grove where you can see the best international designer clothes in Joseph and in the Matches on Ledbury Road. All beyond my means but for a fashion person it is like drinking nectar, just seeing such achingly cool, beautiful stuff. Having lunch or afternoon tea in Daylesford Organic or squeezing downstairs on the communal table at Ottolenghi. All these smart cafés brimming with super-stylish Europeans gives one a sense of being in the heart of Europe. And more recently the arrival of Bill Granger's new London restaurant in Notting Hill, Granger & Co., has brought the best of Australian fresh food to London, with people queuing around the block. No need to wait for my Christmas visit to Sydney to have Bill's ricotta hotcakes with honeycomb butter; somehow they seem even better in Notting Hill.

I loved living in London and friends like the ebullient Craig Markham, who is marketing director of Firmdale Hotels, made it such fun, with all the events and dinners he held at one hotel or another – garden parties in Number Sixteen, dinners in the Soho Hotel, pool parties at the Haymarket Hotel – a memorable one being Kathy Lette's book launch where drag queens performed synchronised swimming. Ah, it reminded me of Sydney! Along with Craig I caught up and hung out with so many of my longstanding London friends – such a talented bunch of interesting people including Marg Caselton, the interior stylist who I first met in Sydney, fashion journalist Andrew Tucker, who I had written alongside at the international shows for years, lifestyle writer Fiona McCarthy who I had met through Craig and my friend Maggie Alderson, journalist turned hugely popular novelist, who lives in a charming cottage in the seaside town of Hastings.

Getting back to work was great. This time it was absolutely a choice, not a life sentence, and that made it all the more appealing. Working with Louise to revamp the magazine was energising and before long I was shooting all the covers, doing all the fashion stories and sundry other features in the magazine. I was back in the saddle and in the time I was at *Good Housekeeping* I styled and directed cover shoots with a whole array of English personalities. Actress Julie Walters was my first cover and what a nice down-to-earth woman she was to deal with. And a great person to start with in England, as she was not the least bit intimidating. Rather more scary was the prospect of shooting a cover and feature with Trinny and Susannah, the most famous stylists in the world at that time. Styling the stylists? What could be more challenging? Especially as Trinny and Susannah were launching their own

SOMERSET HOUSE, WC2
14TH — 18TH SEPTEMBER 2012

Christopher Raeburn — Huishan Zhang
J.JS Lee — JW Anderson
Lucas Nascimento — Marques'Almeida
Michael van der Ham —
Palmer//Harding —
Sister by Sibling —

NEWG
TOP

TOPS

Friends who make my world go around: TOP LEFT TO RIGHT
Fashion writer Andrew Tucker, hotelier Craig Markham
MIDDLE *Beauty editor Elizabeth Barnett; fellow yogi*
Susan Watson. RIGHT *Yoga teacher Lisa Sanfilippo.*

affordable clothing range and the stipulation was that they had to wear their range on the cover. Luckily the shoot with photographer Nicky Johnston went well as he had shot them before. Susannah was quite easy-going but Trinny was more demanding. 'You've got Susannah right because you understand her shape [that is, we are both curvy] but you haven't got me quite right,' she castigated me. I felt like one of the hapless women she styled on their television series. But I held my own and in the end it all looked great and Trinny sent me a note with an overcoat from their new range as a thank-you gift.

My life seemed to go into synchronicity overdrive when I was asked to shoot a cover with Twiggy. This is the face that I plastered over my walls as a teenager in the late 1960s – the iconic Twiggy of *Vogue* cover fame with her huge eyes with big painted lashes and the boyish mod haircut. And I was to do a shoot with her! Twiggy was well and truly back in the British spotlight after Marks and Spencer decided to feature her in their campaigns. Talk about 1960s synchronicity; it was her sixtieth year and about to be my sixtieth year. I'd heard she could get a bit tricky on shoots if the clothes weren't working on her so I went into preparation overdrive. Being a similar age and shape I understood how to dress her. My assistants Lucy and Nini got used to me stripping down to my underwear in the 'fashion cupboard' to try everything on before a shoot to see if it worked. I don't think they'd ever seen a fashion director do that before. So by the time I got to the shoot I had so many outfits ready and sorted, down to the smallest detail. It all went very well and Twiggy was in great form and happy with it all. I kept the whole 1960s mood going for the *Good Housekeeping* cover, shooting her in a white mod chair in a bright orange trench coat.

Over that year Twiggy and I did a number of shoots together for *Good Housekeeping*, along with Brian Aris, her favourite photographer. Chatting on the shoot about modelling and fame Twiggy mused on the fact that both she and Kate Moss had both been told they were too short to be models and yet they had ended up being the most famous

British models of all. For another Twiggy cover, we shot two versions for the cover, one in white tulle skirt with a bit of a nod to Sergeant Pepper, the other in glam black tulle, both with Twiggy swinging in a transparent hanging 1960s chair. The images turned out so well that the *Good Housekeeping* editor decided to use both covers and divided the print run into two. One of Brian's pictures done for the issue of Twiggy wearing the black tulle skirt and leather jacket sitting on the floor in the studio with her shoes off was shown later in London's National Portrait Gallery in an exhibition on Twiggy and it also appeared in the catalogue. This was a great memento melding my two worlds, curatorial and editorial, together.

In just one year in London I seemed to have shot covers with a swathe of Britain's best-known names. There was the challenge of dressing the very curvy and incredibly beautiful Nigella Lawson. She looked luscious spilling out of a couture blush-silk satin corset by Vivienne Westwood and a full skirt. With a real hourglass figure and a marmoreal complexion, Nigella would have been the perfect Edwardian beauty. However, in the 21st century she is a bit of an anachronism and quite difficult to dress at a time when pre-pubescent waifs are worshipped on the altar of fashion. For me she was probably one of the most beautiful women I have ever done as a cover shoot. The only man I styled for *Good Housekeeping* was the adorable and admirable Jamie Oliver, who was like working with an endearing kid with ADD, bouncing around full of energy. He's a hero for introducing good food and cooking to a whole generation of children who can barely recognise a vegetable and I decided to try styling him very differently from his usual casual scruffiness and went for a kind of James Bond sexiness in a Paul Smith tuxedo and loosened bow tie. When I was asked to do a cover shoot with the hapless Duchess of York it was familiar territory, as I'd shot her before for *The Australian Women's Weekly* for two covers. Frenetic but friendly, the Duchess is passionately interested in photography and loves the whole process of doing a shoot. She has an

ABOVE *Sarah Canet at her wedding
in a Collette Dinnigan gown.*

BELOW LEFT *Artist Loene Furler.*

BELOW RIGHT *Photographer Juli Balla
visiting from Oz.*

energetic force field around her that would wear out anyone but the strong. So for the *Good Housekeeping* cover I decided to go with strong, bright greens and violets with bold costume jewellery that worked well with her red hair and perfectly mirrored her big personality.

On the fashion side I created some gorgeous shoots for *Good House-keeping*, doing many in Australia during the summer with my favourite teams when I was out in Christmas to see my family and friends. I shot those with my friend Juli Balla, who has the best eye in the business. For one story we hired a vintage yacht and shot a nautical theme, one of fashion's great perennials, out on Sydney Harbour on a glorious summer's day. On another memorable trip, the *Good Housekeeping* fashion team flew off to Morocco, where the affable Aussie photographer Graham Shearer came from his home in the south of France to shoot in the wonderful crumbling Riad Edward in the midst of the old city where the Muslim call to prayer woke me every morning at dawn. We then drove out in a rickety old van of the city into the countryside and stayed in the fabulous Bab Ourika, an ochre-washed hotel bathed in sunshine that faced the mysterious snow-capped Atlas Mountains. There is nothing I love more than combining style and travel so doing fashion shoots with a great team in a wonderful location is my idea of perfect work. Getting a second chance to do it made me very happy and recaptured the magic of working again. I realised that I'm not good at not working; without a purpose and without people around me I can lapse into depression, as I discovered in Paris.

All was going so well in London. I was incredibly busy and was enjoying working hard again. Louise and I devised new features together for the magazine to celebrate the older woman, who was our primary demographic. I'm passionate about redressing the paucity of older women seen in the media in any way I can. We devised the successful concept of *Good Housekeeping*'s 'Best-dressed list of forty gorgeous women over forty'. It received worldwide attention in the media and my story was quoted from London to New Delhi. This ran in *The Telegraph* in London with a quote from me – 'Jane de Teliga, the magazine's fashion director, said: "Why is it that when Helen Mirren was snapped this summer on the beach sporting a red bikini, it sent shockwaves through the media?"' It was great to be able to use the notion of a best-dressed list to bring home the idea that chic, beautiful women over the age of forty exist and it sure helped that Yasmin Le Bon (who at the time was forty-three) was chosen as our number one on the best-dressed British countdown. The listing also featured the likes of Dame Judi Dench, Joanna Lumley, London-based Australians Elle Macpherson and Kylie Minogue and the wild extremes of British dressing such as the maverick designer Vivienne Westwood with her trademark bright orange hair doing her utmost to age 'disgracefully', and the classic octogenarian icon The Queen.

But suddenly the mood around the world changed as the global financial crisis hit. And it hit the media world hard. Circulation slowed, as did advertising. One Friday it all changed on the magazine when Louise suddenly exited the editorship of *Good Housekeeping*. Louise and I understood each other and worked so well together and I missed that. The former editor of *Good Housekeeping* returned and while she really understood her market in middle England, working with someone who had a headmistress style of management proved to be a challenge for me, as I am a bolshie Australian who does not handle authoritarian direction well. I wanted to stay at least another six months to complete a year and round out my experience in London and I did. Then one day I decided it was time to move on and go freelance, reasoning that I only had one life and there was so much more that I wanted to experience while I was in London and before I got too old to work. The spectre of running out of time haunts me and I genuinely feel lucky to be still working in such an age-conscious industry as fashion. After I left I continued to style celebrities for covers and features for *Good House-keeping* and to do various editing, styling and writing on a freelance basis. A stint editing an issue of the Singaporean in-house magazine

British icons:
TOP *Designer queen, Dame Vivienne Westwood.*
BOTTOM *Flag drapery in The Ritz, London.*

*Seeing spots: Me in Covent Garden at London Fashion Week,
taken by blogger photographer Vanessa Jackman.*

for Club 21 was a learning experience and not a particularly successful one, working far from people in the team. However, styling stories for my old alma mater *The Australian Women's Weekly* was always great as we knew each other so well, so I spent a day shooting with the extraordinary Zandra Rhodes in her home in London and another out-of-the ordinary experience shooting with the Duchess of Rutland in Belvoir Castle, a story that never ran due to a change in editorship. For me spending a day at the castle with the ebullient Emma and her children was a marvellous, unrepeatable experience – where else would you have a duchess in full evening dress up a ladder cleaning the family Holbein portrait with a chook-feather duster? That's the thing about this business I've serendipitously found myself in – people are utterly fascinating and their lives so extraordinary, whether an Aussie farmer looking for a wife or a duchess dusting a national treasure. And I always feel so lucky that I get to see into their world just for a while.

Then something happened to change my world. One day I woke and went online to do some banking and for the first time the bank included my superannuation investment in my accounts. I looked in astonishment and horror. There was a line of numbers that pierced my lungs and left me breathless. I had lost three-quarters of my money. All the money from my house sale, virtually all my superannuation, in fact, nearly all the money I had saved in the world. It had been wiped out by the global financial crisis meltdown from the high-risk investment portfolio that I had been convinced by a financial advisor would be the best for me. It was almost all gone and with it went the future I had imagined. It was a baby-boomer's nightmare. I had envisaged a lovely retirement and little Provençal villa; instead I was looking at a lifetime as a 'distressed gentlewoman' as they used to call them in Victorian England. In shock and feeling distressed, I rang my daughter Emily, and sobbed, 'I am penniless.' To which my practical girl answered in her stern and serious way, 'Mum, no matter what happens you will always have a home and I will always look after you.' Very kind of her but the thought of relying on one's daughter seemed very tragic. It seemed like one of those turning points as you get older when the roles reverse; I was now the child and she was the adult and I found it very unnerving. Despite this uneasiness I knew I would always be in safe hands if my wonderful, capable girls were in charge.

Once the shock had passed, there was nothing to do apart from accept the fact that I had lost my money and to learn to live with less. At the risk of coming over all *Ab Fab*, the thing that really helped me was Buddhist philosophy. For more than a decade I have been reading and studying books on Buddhism and during times when I feel most distressed this is what saves me. In the self-indulgent West, we have an expectation of happiness that will come somehow if we satisfy all our desires. While the Buddhists seek happiness for all sentient beings, they acknowledge that life involves suffering. And that suffering comes largely from constantly craving more. When your job is about fashion and constantly changing desires, this can be a very hard road to travel. The balance between spirituality and materialism is a delicate one for someone whose livelihood depends on a desire for more. But acceptance, no matter what happens, is probably the most important life lesson of all. So, with the devastation of finding out that my financial world order had changed dramatically, I thought about my grandmother, holding her hand as she took her last breath and I realised that, in the end, you just need a roof over your head, a comfortable bed and someone who loves you to hold your hand. All the rest is ultimately superfluous. Gradually the gut-wrenching fear of destitution faded as I repeated this mantra to myself – I just need a bed and people who love me.

Though I have never been wealthy I've always had enough to live life well. In Australia we are mostly used to a very comfortable life, but in London the gap between your earnings and your standard of living is very slim. The cost of living in London, one of the great cities of the world, is high and I had already learnt to pare down my

Seeing red: TOP *My mother forced, by me, to pose in phone box with my friends Andrew Tucker and Dan Silby; London 2010.*

ABOVE RIGHT *Pretty mushroom, Hampstead Heath.*

LEFT *Red double decker in front of the church, St Martins in the Field, Trafalgar Square.*

expectations – less space and less possessions. I was without a car for the first time in a very long time, so I had to learn to embrace public transport and travelling on the tube became second nature. While I had to learn to live with much less, I was comforted by the underlying belief that the universe would provide for me. Having packed up my home and left my old life behind to live in a tiny Paris apartment with few possessions had prepared me for a new way of living with less. My London mentor for living in a new way was my big bear of a friend, Andrew Tucker, who I had known since we sat side by side covering the shows. He teased me constantly about being a princess and questioned my spending. He attacked my 'princessness' with missionary zeal. We went on forays to shop in the many charity shops that are a feature of every British high street. I became much more resourceful and learned to love finding old cutlery and crockery at bargain prices. I drew the line at buying old clothes though as I just cannot stand that old clothes smell. Plus as you get older, wearing vintage that can look so cool on some-body younger just looks like you're stuck in some sad time warp wearing your old clothes. My vintage mostly comes from my own closet. The term 'shopping your closet' became my reality. And it's amazing how resourceful you can become at reworking your wardrobe. Clothes were reworked in different mixes; some clothes that I would have passed on to charity shops were re-tailored or repaired. I started buying only in the twice-yearly sales of the major stores (Fenwick in Bond Street being my absolute favourite hunting ground) and acquiring recycled designer pieces at dress agency boutiques. Handbags that I would have given away in the past to family and friends were dragged out of the top of my wardrobe and reworn. I remember going to a launch in Selfridges and being delighted that Anya Hindmarch commented on how she loved seeing me still wearing one of her old designs.

In keeping with my personal economic rationalisation I moved out of my little studio in Notting Hill and moved into a big old apartment in Maida Vale with my friend Marg Caselton, the inventive and funny interior stylist who had spent some time in Sydney styling for *Vogue Living* and *Vogue Entertaining*. It was like being a young girl sharing a flat with a friend again, yet this time I was in my fifties rather than my twenties. It was so strange to be negotiating each other's quirks and foibles, working out bathroom rituals and food habits with someone who is a friend rather than family. After living on my own for a while, it was not only more economical to share costs; it was also companionable to be able to sit around the dinner table at night and talk about our days. The only downside was it was up four big flights of stairs in a big mansion block, purpose-built during the Edwardian era. Lugging a suitcase up those stairs was heart-attack material, but we used to joke that it saved on gym membership. When Marg moved back to her own house after her tenants left, I went back to Sydney for the summer.

It was heaven to bask in a lovely summer of family, friends and sun and so comforting to hang out with my family – living and laughing with Madeleine and her boyfriend Tim in my old rented apartment which they had taken over, my furniture still in place but overlaid with their quirky conglomeration of stuff such as strange little installations of their own making. Virtually every day Emily came over, often with her boyfriend Adrian and we'd all pootle around, and troop downstairs for delicious meals at my lovely mama's, who rented in the same building. It was our little family compound; my sister Emma was next door and my mother downstairs we would leave the doors unlocked and move from one apartment to another. For a few months I was so happy to be there; however, I really felt now that London was my home and I felt compelled to go back. I searched online for a place to rent of my own in London. After days of searching for something I could afford in an area I wanted to live (location, location, location being an immutable maxim), I saw a shabby apartment with potential, listed in Belsize Village just near Marg's place. I took it sight unseen after Marg reported back, having gone to see it for me, that it was very quirky but she knew I could do something with it.

TOP
Autumn leaves.

BOTTOM
Canal boat, Maida Vale.

TOP
*Chez moi: Above the lovely Belsize
village deli.*

BOTTOM
*My friend Marg Caselton with
her granddaughter Lois.*

Coming back to London to the cold and snow was daunting but the joy of nesting soon absorbed my every waking moment. I arrived and walked into my new apartment. Shabby but freshly painted with wide old floorboards, it was completely empty save for some oddly coloured green venetians and a big Persian rug. Somehow I found that exhilarating! The sum total of my possessions were some books, magazines and papers, my Butterfly lamp from Paris, a helluva lot of clothes and accessories (I'm a fashion editor after all), and the beautiful old rug bursting with cabbage roses that I had bought when I first moved to London. I set about decorating, creating my own kind of *La Bohème* set on a very tight budget. I just loved it. As a stylist it's like creating a set to live in. My friend Andrew again admonished me with 'Being frugal can be a real pleasure' and he was right. I bought an old armchair off the street from my favourite end of Portobello on Golborne Road where tourists rarely venture. I slept on an airbed until I trekked out to Ikea and ordered a spare Gustavian iron bedstead that looked like a 19th-century original, which I covered in a flower-strewn quilt sewn by my mother to my chosen colours and heritage fabrics. Andrew and his partner Dan took me thrift shopping at car boot sales and auctions, and gradually my place took shape. A very girly, bohemian kind of style emerged around me and I loved it. I'd sit on my bed and in a kind of meditation look around me and let my eyes rest on the funny little things I had collected and think 'how pretty'. Marg loved it too and featured it in a shoot for *Good Housekeeping* where she was working as interiors editor. The headline to my story read: 'The surprising pleasures of frugal living', a paraphrase of Andrew's words. Hmmm, not exactly what I would like to read about myself but I've learnt one has to let go of this sort of misplaced pride.

And if there's one mantra I followed through all this change and upheaval, it was 'go with the flow'. And I still kept my belief in the universe providing for me. Despite leaving full-time work, going out on a limb to freelance and the kicker of the global financial crisis on my

ABOVE
*London living: My flat
in Belsize village.*

RIGHT
*Mantlepiece assemblage
with Akira postcard.*

Photos: Polly Eltes

finances, the work kept flowing in. When you release any resistance to what *is* and go with the flow, life becomes easier. As if to reaffirm this I serendipitously rediscovered a book that Michelle Jank had given me when we were both living in Paris. Funny how things come up when the time is right. It was Eckhart Tolle's book *The Power of Now* and it helped greatly to keep things in perspective. There were times when I thought I was going to run out of money and then another job styling or writing would appear. Living like this is probably perfect for someone like me who has a very low boredom threshold. Scary but exciting as I never knew where life would lead me. I have always loved the buzz of doing different things every day. Even though I'd get worried I always tried to stay in the moment and live in the present – a very Buddhist discipline. I've learnt that many of one's worries are in fact projections into the future, which may or may not happen and if you ask yourself 'How is my life right now at this minute?' the answer is often, 'It's just fine.'

Someone suggested me as a celebrity stylist to *Hello* magazine and so another shoot took place with the Duchess of York, who was talking about her financial woes yet again. In the midst of the shoot during a break I rushed into the laundry of the house we were shooting in to get some privacy while I talked to my landlady about my flat and next thing I know the duchess, clearly with the same idea, burst into the laundry clutching one of her many mobiles (which she kept in a kind of plumber's belt and each one with a different ring tone so she knew who was calling). Very bizarre what with me talking to my landlady at one end and the Duchess crouched at another end talking to her daughter Eugenie, both of us among the washing machine, dryer and ironing boards. Who'd have believed it!

Also for *Hello* magazine I spent a day with Jerry Hall, Texan super-model and ex-wife of Mick Jagger, in her Richmond home. I arrived early to be sent away into the drizzle by Jerry until the appointed time. I wandered until I found a café to wait in and when I did get back to her house, I was shown the servant's entrance by the housekeeper. That made me feel very special but I took a deep breath and carried on. The shoot with Brian Aris, who is much loved by baby-boomer stars, was a tad odd. One minute the long, lean siren Jerry, who insisted on doing her own hair and makeup, was posing in an old pair of jeans in her garden clutching a hen to her face to demonstrate her interest in organic home self-sufficiency, the next she was sweeping down the staircase in a Tara-like ensemble and then moving on to a full-blown glamour scene wearing her own fur-trimmed violet Christian Dior ensemble in her vast sitting room. Where, I ask you, would one get to experience this in normal everyday life? The celebrity stylist's working life is 'bonkers', to use one of my favourite English words.

And for something completely different, Andrew, who is course director for MA Fashion Journalism at the prestigious London College of Fashion, asked me to become the external examiner. What I thought would be a brief appointment turned out to be a serious academic four-year stint. It's fascinating seeing how much fashion journalism has changed. Nowadays, a fashion journalist needs to be a writer, stylist, photographer, blogger and even graphic designer. Something I now do in my working life. Some days I wish I could stop the world and get some proper training but it's a headlong rush into the deep end every day.

One thing that I can do standing on my head is lecture about fashion. For many people public speaking is agony; for me it's something, strangely, I enjoy. I love the challenge of holding an audience's attention by entertaining and informing them. One of the memorable lectures I gave was to the Friends of the Victoria and Albert Museum on 'Style Icons of the 20th Century', which was advertised in the Victoria and Albert brochure with a great fashion photo of Twiggy on a bicycle in 1967 by Ronald Traeger. Of course, at one point when I hadn't heard from the Victoria and Albert, I fearfully imagined that perhaps they had virtually no ticket sales and I thought ahead to facing the

Silver screen: Me lecturing at the Victoria & Albert museum, London.

embarrassment of talking to a solitary person in a very empty auditorium. Just when I'd thought the worst, I got a call saying my lecture was completely sold out with a waiting list to attend! It went really well as I packed my talk with fantastic images of the chicest women in the world of the past century and knew my subjects well enough to just glance at my notes to keep me on track and make a few funny comments. Sometimes I'm not sure from one moment to the next what is going to pop out of my mouth. This is a way to surprise and hold your audience that I've learnt from years of public speaking. Afterwards, buzzing with the rush of the talk, I even had some of the audience coming up to say how much they enjoyed it, something very unusual from the normally reticent English.

The academic turn in my career continued when I was asked to lecture in the Fashion Styling degree at Southampton Solent University. Clementine, my former assistant, had gone on to work as a senior lecturer there and, in one of those strange twists, which seems like a baby-boomer movie plot, we swapped places. She became my boss! What started out as a day here and there grew each year into a big commitment that now sees me as a full-time senior lecturer. That's a whole other story but more of that later.

Adaptability became the key to my life in London as I flowed from one thing to another. I continued to cover London Fashion Week for *The Australian* newspaper. Friends laughed when an invitation arrived addressed to 'Jane de Teliga, *The Australian*'. My twin loves of fashion and travel floated along happily beside each other, as I was asked, via my friend Maggie Alderson, to join a group of writers doing pieces on their personal travel experiences for the website called www.holiday-goddess.com The proactive astrologer Jessica Adams has marshalled 30 writers from all around the world to write for this website to help fellow female travellers on their journeys. So into the brave new world of cyberspace I journeyed.

And at the same time I began my own foray into the web world.

One day I was talking to my friend Elizabeth Barnett, who resembles a beautiful Victorian doll with her round face and huge blue eyes, about what we were both doing as freelancers. After much chat, we decided to start a business together. What if we took our magazine skills into the real world as a stylist and beauty editor? We could edit people's wardrobes, go shopping with them and come up with a personalised beauty/fashion regime for women who wanted some extra advice in that department. We created a personal styling business, which we named Style on Call and we set up a website. The only money we had to put up was for our website, reasoning that at the very least we would have a beautiful website for people to look through. This venture was a huge learning curve for both of us and we got great publicity but in the midst of the recession, it really didn't make us a whole lot of money. Rather than being defeated, we adjusted our focus and adapted it into a consultancy and dropped the personal styling altogether. I started a blog on the website, which I still do update every season during London Fashion Week at www.styleoncall.co.uk. It is my very first blog and a whole cyberspace world opened up for me. One morning I woke up and looked at my personal emails, then our business emails, then my Facebook page, the business Facebook page then Linked-in, then my Twitter page and the business Twitter page. Arrgh, I thought my head would blow off! Maggie Alderson, who is a marvel in the early adoption of new media, was an inspiration in that department.

While I was battling the blog, another big project came up editing the book *My Style* by Dannii Minogue for Simon & Schuster. Danni, whose appearance on *The X Factor* had raised her to superstardom in Britain, worked personally on all aspects of the book. This was no walk in and walk out scenario; Dannii, in her hardworking and driven way, had lots of ideas and wanted it to be a very practical and very visual magazine-style book. After talking to Dannii and the publishers, I created the concept for the book and outlined what each chapter would contain. With this as a template, Danni ran with it, working with her

My shot of Dannii Minogue being photographed by Jonty Davies for her book
My Style *at the Soho Hotel, London.*

friend, the clever wordsmith Charlotte James to create it. Art Director Nikki Dupin, who was a dream to work with, designed the book and we produced it in record time. What made the book so beautiful was the gorgeous shoot we did for it with Dannii in London. Dannii had flown to London and unbeknown to her at the time she was not well, finding out later that she was suffering from a thyroid condition after the birth of her baby son. She was feeling fragile and just as we were about to shoot she was taken to hospital with appendicitis. Being the show-must-go-on kind of a gal, we did an amazing shoot the following week with English photographer Jonty Davies who had shot her before for *Marie Claire*. It all took place in the fabulous penthouse apartment at the Soho Hotel in London, with acres of rooms with fabulous decor and a balcony that ran right around it. It was a fashion stylist's dream shoot to work on.

It was while I was holding a small party in my London flat that I realised how far I'd come and how much happier and more comfortable in my own skin I was at this time in my life. Yes, I had run away to Paris and experienced *la vie Parisienne* and also survived some down times, my fair share of lonely, sad days and the financial woes in London but I'd also prospered and found a new, unexpected way of living. There in that funny boho Belsize pad were my close friends, new and old, Australian, English and American, of all ages. We laughed as I fooled around with a hideous kangaroo paw bottle opener Andrew had bought me as a joke housewarming present, sticking it up my sleeve and someone shoved a cigarette in it. I realised I was really happy and that I had created a new life for myself and I felt so very lucky. The work, so wonderfully varied, kept coming, and a testament to the concept of going with the flow – long may it continue. And miracle of miracles, after some very kind legal help, the bank had restituted some of my lost superannuation. I was full of gratitude for my life.

For me, London is the best city in the world; there is so much to do or see there that you just never ever get to the end of it. For those

TOP *Flying the flag.*
ABOVE *London view from Primrose Hill.*
RIGHT *Window at VV Rouleaux, Marylebone.*

baby-boomers who remember the grungy, grubby city of the 1970s with the bad food and even worse weather, London is so much more beautiful now and has become an exciting European city. In London I feel I am truly a part of the world around me, unlike Paris where I felt I was watching from the sidelines. I'm involved in London in every way professionally and socially. It feels like home. The oft-quoted words of Samuel Johnson still ring true centuries later, 'When a man is tired of London, he is tired of life; for there is in London all that life can afford.' I am no longer tired of life!

WHAT I'VE LEARNT ABOUT

LIVING WITH LESS

———

Moving to the other side of the world with just two suitcases (albeit the size of two small lorries, as my sister Sarah says) taught me how to live with less. Basically I went from being a comfortable, relentlessly middle-class woman with her own home and own car to learning how to live like a cash-strapped student again. Living in a tiny apartment of two rooms plus a bathroom, with very few possessions, was so freeing. There's very little to clean, and almost no clutter. I was surprised how little I missed all the stuff that surrounded me in my old life. And when you do buy something for the home, like some new bed linen, it's so exciting you really appreciate it.

✳

WHAT I'VE LEARNT ABOUT

SHOPPING FOR CLOTHES ON A LIMITED BUDGET

—

No matter what the language, the one word that gladdens the hearts of women the world over is 'sales/*soldes*/*saldi*'. Nowadays sales come around so fast you are still in the middle of the season in which you can wear the clothes. But set rules for yourself beforehand. Planning what I 'need' in my wardrobe rather than what I just 'want' helps focus my shopping as does checking out the stores just beforehand. The best is seeing something I longed for earlier at full price, on sale. Then it's a no-brainer to buy. Much of my best pieces come from Fenwick Bond Street, which has the best sales ever. One great jacket I first saw when it was over £600; I bought it on its second markdown for £99. It was rather too big but I had a tailor perfect the fit.

WHAT I'VE LEARNT ABOUT

CULLING MY WARDROBE

———

And talking of languishing, cull your wardrobe regularly. Get a friend to help. I find a ruthless daughter works very well. My oldest daughter Emily is a master at the wardrobe cull and has an eagle fashion eye. I have to plead the case of threatened items. Some of her memorable comments in the past have included such gems as 'you look like a burns victim in that', referring to a tight-fitting clingy top in a nude colour. I once previewed a colourful patchwork trench and silk pants that I was planning to wear to open a major exhibition at the National Portrait Gallery in Canberra. Her comment? 'Who do you think you are? Santa's little helper?' I still wore it and included her comment in my speech – it got a great laugh and helped me get over the nerves of speaking in front of 400 people.

The one thing I know for sure is that is does matter what you wear. You tell a story about yourself every time you walk out the door so make it say what you want it to say. We are so lucky that as women we can create that story anew every day.

＊

USING A GOOD TAILOR

———

A really good tailor or alterations person can make a world of difference. In my more straitened financial times, I 'shop my closet'. Things that I would have given, in my former life, to friends, family or charity shops I rework and have altered. Anything that needed repairing or simply had something that stopped me wearing it, I got tailored. I once spent £200 doing this and it felt like I had a whole new set of clothes. Nothing languishes in the wardrobe taking up space and confusing the issue; everything has to work hard and for the first time in my adult life things have actually worn out. A very novel occurrence for a fashion editor.

✳

SOURCING SECOND-HAND HOMEWARES

———

In London I found brilliant bits and pieces for my home at one of the myriad charity stores that line every high street. British Heart Foundation or Oxfam are great for home finds, from casserole dishes to glasses or books. I can't come at the charity shop clothes unless I go to Mary's Living and Giving in Primrose Hill (where I've donated clothes). When I have had the money to upgrade, I just take stuff back to the charity stores and let the process begin again. Feel-good factor all round.

I'll never buy new again, as far as decorating is concerned, after going to auction houses in London (Chiswick Auctions with my friends Andrew and Dan), and finding beautiful furniture, porcelain and paintings. Not only is it the best fun ever, it's surprisingly inexpensive as well as being a great learning experience. It's often cheaper than Ikea and you're buying beautiful antique wooden pieces, not flat-pack wibble-wobble. You do wonder why you ever bought new furniture for full price before. The exceptions are beds and for that I've found Ikea mattresses and beds are really very comfortable.

*

THE LISTING
PLACES I LOVE TO SHOP
(OR WINDOWSHOP)

I've rediscovered London in the time that I've lived here. Plus, now that I've learned to love the city's public transport system, I've made some wonderful finds – some secret local haunts and some not-so-secret London legends that I love to visit.

For the full shopping experience there's Selfridges on Oxford Street, so large it is practically a town in itself, or go to Knightsbridge for the Ab Fabulousness of Harvey Nichols, and the favourite of Arab princesses and well-heeled tourists, the one and only Harrods.

My favourite shopping area in London is Notting Hill's Westbourne Grove and Ledbury Road. A super-smart swag of shops for the international set and local yummy mummies. Visit Joseph for top designer names plus their own brand offerings and check out their shoe store in Ledbury Road. Go to Matches for great designer clothes and accessories and nip across the street for the younger, less expensive collections. Visit the English middle-class staples of Jigsaw and LK Bennett or go French with a row of many hip brands all in a row – Sandro, Maje, Zadig & Voltaire, and Loft are my picks for cool basics.

BROWNS

www.brownsfashion.com
24–27 South Molton Street
London W1K 5RD
Telephone: +44 (0) 20 7514 0016

Started by the legendary Joan Burstein, Browns is a cluster of townhouses filled with the best international designer names. A small but eye-boggling fine jewellery department (with treasures by my favourite London jeweller Ram) makes it a must-see.

COS

www.cosstores.com
222 Regent Street,
London, W1B 5BD
Telephone: +44 (0) 20 7478 0400

The grown-up version of the high street fave H&M, with cool clothes that work for all ages.

DAUNT BOOKS

www.dauntbooks.co.uk
83–84 Marylebone High Street
London W1U 4QW
Telephone: +44 (0) 20 7224 2295

A delicious travel and literary bookshop housed in a beautiful vintage-looking store, with other smaller and lovely branches dotted around London including Belsize Village and Hampstead.

DESIGNS

60 Rosslyn Hill
Hampstead, NW3 1ND
Telephone: +44 (0) 20 7435 0100

My secret squirrel designer boutique
with top labels recycled by the well-
heeled locals. Depends on the day as
with all dress agencies but not unusual
to find hardly worn pieces by Lanvin,
Dries van Noten or Donna Karan. Now
you know, I may have to 'keel' you.

DOVER STREET MARKET

www.doverstreetmarket.com
17–18 Dover Street
London W1S 4LT
Telephone: +44 (0) 20 7518 0680

Owned by Comme des Garçons, this
is the ultimate in exclusive designer
shopping with a curated collection of
offerings by Alaïa, Celine, Lanvin, Yves
Saint Laurent and new Brit designers
like Mary Katranzou. Once, foraging
through the racks, I turned to find the
beautiful Queen Rania of Jordan beside
me. This is my 'dream' shopping venue,
as in 'in your dreams'.

FENWICK BOND STREET

www.fenwick.co.uk/bond-street
63 New Bond Street
London W1A 3BS
Telephone: +44 (0) 20 7629 9161

This is a big favourite of mine. It's
a delightful, peaceful small department
store where women, particularly a chic
woman of a certain age, can find smart
clothes without the usual frump factor
by designers from around the world.
I love afternoon tea there in Bond and
Brook café, particularly the dainty fruit
scones with their own jam and clotted

cream. Yum. All in all a grown-up
girly experience.

HARRODS

www.harrods.com
87–135 Brompton Road
Knightsbridge
London SW1X 7XL
Telephone: +44 (0) 20 7730 1234

Looking smarter by the minute
since new Arab owners bought it;
big designer boutiques and still
those famous, fabulous sales.

HARVEY NICHOLS

www.harveynichols.com
109–125 Knightsbridge
London SW1X 7RJ
Telephone: +44 (0) 20 7235 5000

Of *Ab Fab* fame, 'Harvey Nicks' is
a treat for fashion fiends. I love the
jewellery concessions on the ground
floor such the Talisman gallery,

JOSEPH

www.joseph.co.uk
230–236 Westbourne Grove
London, Greater London W11 2RH
Telephone: +44 (0) 20 7243 9920

International designer dreams in dress
and the more affordable Joseph own
label stocked together in an airy store.

LIBERTY

www.liberty.co.uk
Regent Street
London W1B 5AH
Telephone: +44 (0) 20 7734 1234

A jewel of a department store in
a heritage building which has been

voted for many years running by *Time Out* as the best shop in London. I browse for hours in the jewellery, beauty and accessories on the ground floor.

LOFT DESIGN BY . . .

www.loftdesignby.com
86 Westbourne Grove
Notting Hill W11 2
Telephone: +44 (0) 20 7221 5666

Chic French easy luxe basics such as fine cashmere knits and great T-shirts.

MASSIMO DUTTI

www.massimodutti.com
315-319 Oxford Street
London W1
Telephone: +44 (0) 20 7917 9130

Neo-preppy Spanish tailoring at high street prices by the people who own high street chain Zara. I can't get enough of their knits or leather pieces.

MATCHES

www.matchesfashion.com
60–64 Ledbury Road
Notting Hill W11 2AJ
Telephone: +44 (0) 20 7221 0255

An edited selection of some of the most fashion forward labels to lust after for any serious fashionista.

PORTOBELLO MARKET

www.portobellomarket.org
www.portobelloroad.co.uk/
Portobello Road, Notting Hill,
London W11

Portobello Market is my all-time favourite place to go in London on a Saturday; it is crazily busy and not for the faint-hearted but alive with people, antiques, music, food, second-hand clothes and furniture. Go right to the end to the shabby but fast-gentrifying Golborne Road where the locals like to hang out.

SELFRIDGES & CO

www.selfridges.com
400 Oxford Street
London W1A 1AB
Telephone: +44 (0) 11 3369 8040

So big it is practically a town all of its own with a massive shoe department that stretches across a city block.

UNIQUE PROFESSIONAL TAILORING

15 Flask Walk
Hampstead NW3 1HJ
Telephone: +44 (0) 20 7431 3314

A fantastic Turkish tailor, who has been re-tailoring designer pieces for me for some years with great success.

VV ROULEAUX

www.vvrouleaux.com
102 Marylebone Lane
London W1U 2QD
Telephone: (0) 20 7224 5179

A trove of ribbons, trimmings and flowers for DIY devotees. Browse Marylebone Lane, which is a hidden gem full of little stores, such as quaint old-fashioned deli Paul Rothe & Sons, which looks like something from wartime London.

PLACES I LOVE TO EAT

ANDREW EDMONDS

46 Lexington Street
Soho London W1F 0LW

I love this little Dickensian restaurant
in the heart of Soho with its modern
British food. It's one of Soho's stalwarts
that hasn't changed for years.

BELSIZE KITCHEN

www.belsizekitchen.co.uk
68 Belsize Lane
Belsize Village, NW3 5BJ
Telephone: +44 (0) 20 7794 6957

My local in London for best value
breakfasts and lunches by New
Zealander Adrian Stoddard, who knows
fresh produce when he sees it. In the
charming Belsize village area, much
loved by its inhabitants.

DAYLESFORD ORGANIC

www.daylesfordorganic.com
Farmshop and Café
208–212 Westbourne Grove
Notting Hill London W11 2RH
Telephone: +44 (0) 20 7313 8050

I love to buy their organic food rather
than eat there because the service is
so frustrating, but their produce
is delicious.

GINGER & WHITE

www.gingerandwhite.com
4a–5a Perrin's Court
Hampstead NW3 1QS
Telephone: (0) 20 7431 9098

Antipodean coffee aficionados get their
fix here in a quaint little cobbled lane
off Hampstead High Street.

GRANGER & CO (AKA BILLS)

grangerandco.com
175 Westbourne Grove
Notting Hill London W11 2SB
Telephone: +44 (0) 20 7229 9111

Nothing beats Australian Bill Granger's
fresh fabulous food and this London
outpost of Bill's is even better. Be
prepared to queue for some time.

MELROSE & MORGAN

www.melroseandmorgan.com
Oriel Hall, Oriel Place
Hampstead NW3 1QN
Telephone: +44 (0) 20 7794 6727

Tasty but pricy takeaway from this
gourmand's delight with a tiny
mezzanine for eating in.

OTTOLENGHI

www.ottolenghi.co.uk
63 Ledbury Road
London W11 2AD
Telephone: +44 (0) 20 7727 1121

Deliciously inventive salads and cakes
to take away or you can try and cram
yourself downstairs at the big table.
Also in Kensington and Islington.

ROSE'S BAKERY AT DOVER STREET MARKET

17–18 Dover Street
London W1S 4LT
Telephone: +44 (0) 20 7518 0680

Reluctant as I am to reveal it, this is my secret squirrel place to eat lunch in London. It's a tiny space, a tiny menu but delicious 'home' style cooking. I've recommended Rose's Bakery in Paris, too.

THE WELLS

www.thewellshampstead.co.uk
30 Well Walk
London NW3 1BX
Telephone: +44 (0) 20 7794 3785

A favourite place to go after walking on Hampstead Heath, this friendly gastro-pub has a pub downstairs and a fancier restaurant upstairs (oddly all the same prices). President Obama visited here when he was last in London.

XO

www.rickerrestaurants.com
29 Belsize Lane
Belsize Village, London NW3 5AS
Telephone: +44 (0) 207 433 0888

A cool urban bar and Asian restaurant, owned by expat Aussie Will Ricker, where you can quaff excellent cocktails and great Asian tapas in the bar or eat a full meal in the restaurant. The small cafe next door is popular for coffee and take-away. Sister restaurant E&O is a Notting Hill favourite.

PLACES I LOVE TO GO

BOROUGH MARKET

www.boroughmarket.org.uk
8 Southwark Street
London, SE1 1TL
Telephone: +44 (0) 20 7407 1002

London's best-known food market is brimming with wonderful British and international produce. Buy to take away or eat at one of the many stalls, cafes and bars. The best toasted cheese sandwich I have ever eaten can be found there at Kappacasein.

HAMPSTEAD HEATH

www.cityoflondon.gov.uk/things-to-do/green-spaces/hampstead-heath

A day spent on wonderful and ancient Hampstead Heath is like a day in the woodlands of the English countryside. John Keats composed poetry here, Karl Marx brought his family here and John Constable painted bucolic scenes here. The quaint but murky bathing ponds (one for women, one for men and one mixed) are a strange leftover of another century.

National Portrait Gallery

www.npg.org.uk
St Martin's Place
London, WC2H 0HE
Telephone: +44 (0) 20 7306 0055

A fascinating collection of British portraits covering centuries from Tudor times to now. It's one of my favourite museums to visit especially for special exhibitions, from the fleshy portraits of Lucien Freud to holographic photographs of the Queen.

Sir John Soane's Museum

www.soane.org
13 Lincoln's Inn Fields
London, WC2A 3BP
Telephone: +44 (0) 20 7405 2107

A wonderfully idiosyncratic museum that shows the incredible home and collections of architect Sir John Soane, who lived at the turn of the 18th and 19th centuries.

Tate Modern

www.tate.org.uk/visit/tate-modern
Bankside
London SE1 9TG
Telephone: +44 (0) 20 78878752

Arising Phoenix-like from a massive old power station, the Tate Modern is one of the great collections of modern art and a venue for some of the intriguing exhibitions and projects by contemporary artists from around the world.

Victoria and Albert Museum

www.vam.ac.uk
Cromwell Road, London SW7 2RL
Telephone: +44 (0) 20 7942 2000

The wonderful Victoria and Albert Museum is the great decorative arts museum of the world. It is a cornucopia of delights including the newly renovated fashion gallery and has a brilliant shop.

I also love farmer's markets and you can find these dotted all over London, my favourites being in Notting Hill, Marylebone and Hampstead Heath.

ABOVE
*Romance of the rose: Me at Sarah
Canet's wedding in London 2012.*

RIGHT
Venice Giardini.

CHAPTER FIVE

Love, heartache
AND THE WHOLE
DAMN THING

A few romantic adventures

I always thought that by the time I reached my sixties, the love thing would be all sorted out and I'd be living happily ever after in a villa in Italy or my little château in the south of France with a handsome man. Nope, that's not quite the way it's panned out. *Pas de tout*! Instead I found myself living in my little bohemian garret in London in my little *La Bohème* scenario – on my own. I wasn't exactly starving and my tiny hand wasn't frozen (the central heating was doing just fine) but none of it resembled a villa or chateau of any description and there was no debonair silver fox beside me. However, I was happy and pretty content with my life. Surprisingly, I didn't really feel the lack. I was living the life I wanted and there was so much to absorb me that my life felt complete.

It took me a long time to even think about dating again (such a quaint word, 'dating', so very 1950s Americana). Since my somewhat catastrophic relationship in Australia before I left, I had not 'dated' and most definitely had not had a relationship of any kind for quite a few years. Strangely, being on my own for five years just happened and it hardly worried me, as my life was so full of change and interest. Then one fine day I woke up (yes, another of my morning epiphanies) and said to myself, 'Right, that is enough, it's time to meet someone', despite the fact that the underlying thought of getting undressed in front of someone was vaguely alarming. Talking to a few baby-boomer friends, I discovered they also approached this situation with just a touch of fear and dread. One friend sent me an email where she said, '. . . he's asked if I would like to go away for a weekend. Help!!' Just the thought galvanised me into action and I went on my first ever diet, the Dukan diet, which I read the Middleton family had gone on before the royal wedding and they looked pretty good. Up until my late forties I had been a slim person who could eat almost anything, so going on a diet of any sort required the kind of herculean discipline that I had little experience of, or natural aptitude for that matter. Not to mention my love of good food, which wasn't exactly compatible with dieting.

I find gyms ghastly so it was time to ramp up my yoga practice, and Triyoga in Primrose Hill was just ten minutes walk away. Not that I was keen to be as skinny as I used to be when I was younger. I really do think a bit of weight as you get older is more flattering, but one has to draw the line at a spare tyre around the middle. There's nothing alluring about that.

The next thing I did, after much discussion and cajoling from my friends, was to sign on to a dating website, which I did with much trepidation and embarrassment. Putting yourself out there is a scary thing and it all seems a bit tragic to have to advertise yourself, but it has become not only acceptable but also an effective way to meet people. Stories of women meeting their match online have become the stuff of legend. And it's not like we, as single older women, feel comfortable hanging out in bars. (Well, I suppose we could, but the men we meet there may not be not be quite what we are hoping for.)

If you have never signed up for a dating site, brace yourself. First, you have to find photos of yourself that you are happy to have on the website, then there is the daunting task of describing yourself with enough humility to make you sound appealing. I had my dear thirty-something friend Lisa read my first effort and she said it sounded nothing like me. It was all a bit stiff, lacked humour and I gave nothing away of myself. Many drafts submitted for her approval later and there it was, up and running. I learnt from reading the profiles of men online that a bit of humour goes a long way and to stay away from platitudes at all costs. Once you've signed onto the site, it becomes a nerve-racking roller-coaster ride. Suddenly there may be a lot of interest but much of it fizzles out and you are left with a few stayers and a few dates. People you imagine would be great to meet totally ignore you, and some totally unsuitable ones contact you. There were many much younger men who appeared as fans on my page and I puzzled over what they were looking for. A cougar? A sugar mummy? Or just good old no-strings-attached, no-ticking-clock sex? Personally, at this stage in my life, I had zero interest in going there. All I wished for was to find an interesting partner, a fun companion, a caring lover and a best friend in one person. Not much to ask for!

You really have to gird your loins and be prepared for rejection when you join a dating website. You have to finally pluck up the courage to contact someone. A South African woman friend told me, 'You must be proactive' and recounted meeting her partner on a date. And she insisted you have to contact and go out with lots of people because you never know. Eeek! That's when I discovered I am, somewhere in my head, a child of the fifties and that the thought of making the first move was an appalling prospect. Some strange mixture of pride and fear of rejection gripped me. I'm brave and bold about so many things in my life but when it comes to men my courage fails me. And each time I was brave and it failed to get a response I'd feel rejected. But you have to pick yourself up again. I'd never done the dating thing when I was young. There had always been a steady boyfriend for years at a time from the age of sixteen onwards, so dating at fifty-nine was a truly alarming prospect. Watching *Sex and the City* ('So what are we going to do? Sit around bars, sipping Cosmos and sleeping with strangers when we're eighty?' to quote Carrie) or *Bridget Jones' Diary* (who could forget the 'mummy pants'?), had really been my only education as far as dating was concerned! And then there were the stories from other friends.

One friend made me laugh so much when she called Guardian Soulmates, (the popular dating site linked to *The Guardian* newspaper) the 'Guardian soul destroyers' as she was telling me about her experiences on the site. In six months she only got asked out on one date right at the bitter end when she was about to give up. She did go out with this 'date' for a year but they split up with some heartache involved.

One early memorable Internet date I had was with an American guy, who met me for lunch in Primrose Hill at my suggestion at the Greek favourite, Lemonia. From the £9.95 lunch special, he chose the soup for £4.95 and later accepted my money to cover my food. See, dining out in Primrose Hill is not all glamour and celebrity sightings of Sienna Miller and Jude Law. It was a particularly special moment when he pulled out a folder with detailed plans and specs for the composting toilet that he planned to put in for his French cottage and conversation over lunch involved letting me know how the whole system would work. Not the most alluring first date and it was definitely the last with him – even if he did have a French cottage somewhere.

The surprising thing was as soon as I went on the website I also began to meet other people not on the website. The new age adage of 'Put your intention out into the universe and it will return it' seems true for both men and parking spots!

There was B, an international film producer with a narcissistic streak a mile wide, and so funny he talked in brilliant quotable quotes like a Woody Allen character or maybe more like Larry David.

We met on a blind date set up by my friend Saska, who told me she had met this really interesting guy in a Parisian bar in the Marais and had asked if he was single and would he like to meet someone in London. It's really rare for anybody to actually do this; say 'you should meet this guy' and do something about it – so big brownie points to Saska as she really is that kind of 'can-do' gal. Yes, was his answer and so it came to pass. First date organised over the phone with me squirming on the other end trying to sound nonchalant. Aside from the embarrassing false start when he started talking to the wrong woman at the bar while I was watching from a table nearby not knowing what to do, it all went very well. Eventually I caught his eye and he realised he was talking to the wrong woman and what followed was a fun night talking rapid fire back and forth, and laughing. He proved to be quick and funny.

At the end of the night I remember thinking this could be possible. I must have said it out loud because he came back quick as a flash, 'Honey, this wasn't just possible, it was inevitable.' But it wasn't exactly

a whirlwind romance. It became clear that B just wanted a casual relationship and, in some strange way, that freed me to just go with it all.
For him it was the law of least effort. If I was around when it worked
for him, fine, if not it was radio silence. He lived between London
and Paris, so when I was over in Paris we would meet up or he would
meet me when he was in London. With my Catholic upbringing, the
notion that you could sleep with someone without being in love was
still foreign to me. But I was learning a whole new way of behaving,
a kind of non-attachment that made it possible. Something that men
appear to manage but women with their attachment hormones (or is it
simply social conditioning?) find harder. On one of my visits to Paris
we met up and I stayed over at his quaint little apartment in Marais.
The next day he must have found me irritating as he said 'Honey,
you're a pain in the arse.' I retaliated with 'Oh for god's sake, it's like
being with an eighteen-year-old boy'. He practically skipped with joy
replying 'Honey, I know you are trying to insult me but that's the best
compliment I have ever had!' He said to me later that he had told all of
his male friends and they loved it. Silly, silly boys!

B loved the idea that I was writing a book and was plotting his role
in it with true moviemaker enthusiasm. Waking up one morning in my
apartment in London he strutted around the room like some crazed
naked satyr saying, 'So, Honey, am I chapter twelve and thirteen?'
I laughed so much. The man's ego had no bounds! But he could always
make me laugh and I was kind of proud of the fact that this was the first
relationship I'd ever had without any serious commitment involved.

At the time I was so delighted with being thinner that I was getting
a little too enthusiastic with my first ever diet. One big plus was I had
lost all my cravings for sugar but gradually and most uncharacteristi-
cally I also wasn't that fussed about food in general. One evening we set
off for dinner at The Wells, one of my favourite gastropubs in Hampstead. We were running late and rushing up Hampstead High Street;
I stopped for a moment to check out some Tom Ford sunglasses in

Urban country: The Wells Tavern, Hampstead.

a shop window. (Yes, I do remember what label they were.) Suddenly I was sliding down the glass and my world went black; very, very black. I awoke to find myself lying flat on the pavement. People came from everywhere. A kind New Zealand woman came from her apartment over the road and put a pillow under my head; a lovely woman doctor stopped and held my hand. B stood around wringing his hands and complaining about the speed of the ambulance arrival. Finally it came. So I'm lying on the pavement and the ambulance driver, after ascertaining I'm okay, crouches down beside me, no not to minister to me, in fact he pulls out a long form and a pen and gets down to the paperwork. (In England there is always paperwork and it doesn't matter if you are lying in the middle of the pavement on a busy street, it must be done.) When he gets to the question, 'How old are you?' I can remember thinking, 'Oh shit, B, doesn't know how old I am!' And then thinking, 'Well, I can't lie, they might disqualify me from NHS. 'Sixty-one' I said, very quietly through gritted teeth. And in that instant, B got to know that I was a few years older than him. Finally they carted me away in the ambulance and B and I had an exciting sojourn in Accident and Emergency at the hospital. There I asked B to ring my wonderful friend, an ex-nurse from America, Susan Watson, who lived nearby and she came over straight away. While I was being examined by a serious young doctor, B and Susan chatted away in the same room as if they were at a cocktail party. All three proceeded to round on me and give me a stern warning about the evils of dieting and then I was free to go. Later B and I had a very late bite of dinner where he came out with one of his signature remarks, 'Honey, I've got to start dating younger women.' Outrageous but I had to laugh.

After not seeing each other for several months, as we were both off with our respective families, me for Christmas in Sydney, him in LA, he sent me a brief email out of the blue. It included one of his classic pieces of narcissism, with the words, 'I'm glad to know I can still make women swoon.' Back in London he suddenly texted me, wanting to catch up again. Sure,' I texted back, 'but I'm still a pain in the arse!' Quick as a flash came his reply, 'So am I.' A day later while catching up, he was again musing on his starring role in my book, he turned to me in the street and said, 'So Honey . . . umm international film producer . . . so could I have more hair and a bigger c—k?' 'What!' I spluttered in convent girl gasps, 'That's not what I'm putting in my book. My daughters will never forgive me.' B answered, 'Honey, sex sells!' So especially for B, here is the mention of sex and him in my book. Really though, the relationship had reached the point where it either moved up a notch or petered out. I wasn't really cut out for this desultory type of involvement, even though I gave it my best shot. After a few more dates, it just tailed off with no drama. But B helped re-introduce me to the world of dating and who could forget those one-liners!

My London life sped by, full of friends, wonderful events, and lots of travel. This was the life I had imagined for myself when I contemplated running away from home. I gave up on the whole dating thing – it seemed too much hard work for little reward. And on the actual work front there was so much to do: reporting London Fashion Week, developing our Style on Call business and the major contract of creating and editing the book *My Style: Dannii Minogue* for Simon & Schuster. From London it was so blissfully easy to travel to Europe so I went off to Italy at Easter time to meet up with my friend Mary and her family, and to Paris to spend time with Alexandra and Philip, my dear friends from Sydney, and then with Lisa, my yoga teacher and friend, to Turkey on a yoga retreat she was leading.

Summer in Turkey and I was feeling happy, healthy and fit, basking in the sun on the heavenly edge of a turquoise inlet aptly named Paradise Bay. This paradise also became the scene of a burgeoning crush on a chunky European man, who I first met on a yoga retreat a year before. It's not often you find a silver-haired man at yoga so he stood out among the middle-aged women and agile slips of things who usually frequent

In the pink: Shoot with Megan Gale for Pink Ribbon *magazine
with Juli Balla.*

such retreats. Every day we all woke up to an early yoga session on a terrace with breathtaking views across the bay, followed by a hearty breakfast and then a lot of lolling around by the water, then more yoga with dinner to end the day. Between long conversations and diving into the limpid sea, he and I got to know each other and the information that he had split up with his girlfriend was positively thrilling. Oh, if I had only known how she would figure in my life later.

Anyway off I went to Sydney to do a shoot with Megan Gale for *The Australian Women's Weekly* for a special tenth anniversary issue of the Pink Ribbon magazine, which raises funds for breast cancer research. A few sweet emails flew my way from the European 'silver fox' with wonderful photographs taken on the retreat. On my return to London, my fellow yogi and I caught up for a walk to Hampstead Heath, which was followed by an early dinner in a lovely pub. It was a friendly, chaste evening getting to know each other but next morning all hell broke loose. Emails, threats and phone calls from the gentleman's ex-girlfriend began first thing that morning and hounded me for days. The very uneasy sense of being stalked was heightened when she turned up at my yoga class looking for me. It was only that in the middle of the class that I realised who she was when Lisa asked her name. My eyes widened in a silent message to Lisa and I had to be smuggled out the door later to avoid 'the stalker' lying in wait for me. She began trawling through Lisa's yoga teaching schedule all around London searching for me. Despite this most inauspicious scenario a romance ensued with an impossibly wonderful weekend in Venice, the most romantic city in the world. We walked for hours alongside the magical canals in the steamy heat, hopped on and off the vaporettos that ferry you through the ancient breathtakingly beautiful waterways lined with crumbling palazzos. We spent a fascinating day at the Biennale and dined in an adorable trattoria and stayed in a charming little hotel. It was just so lovely – until my mobile phone rang unexpectedly. I showed the phone to my silver-haired gentleman to ask him why his home phone number was ringing me when he was right beside me.

Why indeed? The only explanation was that his ex still had the keys to his house, which raised the question – why? Too many unanswered questions but one thing seemed certain: the 'ex' was not 'ex' enough.

Returning to London after our romantic sojourn (not taking into account the strange phone calls) the silver-haired one succumbed to the madness and called it quits on our burgeoning relationship. I cried over my computer and it was all very reminiscent of the scene where Diane Keaton sobs while writing her play in the middle-aged romantic movie *Something's Gotta Give*. When I saw the film I thought that particular scenario was quite ridiculous. Yet here I was behaving exactly like it, mooning around the house sighing and crying. Why haven't they invented a cure for such madness? Just a tiny chemical cocktail that could change your brain chemistry in a flash.

My antidote for this infuriating 'illness' ran the gamut from playing very loud hip-hop and dancing like a crazed woman round my living room or lying in bed listening to a soothing guided meditation. Emotional eating was out of the question as I had spent the good part of a year struggling to lose eight kilos so I wasn't about to undo the hard work. But a bloody good chocolate brownie or mega cookie (a Daylesford organic Anzac biscuit was my weapon of choice) was so very soothing at times. As for drinking, I've never been any good at that since my first experience when I was nineteen and have virtually never drunk again. Binge clothes buying was tempting but it meant that I would be on the slippery slope to financial ruination. My friends were great during this time but I did spend so much time talking about my romantic misfortune that I became seriously worried that they might have me committed. So walking, meditation, dancing and yoga were my cures. Mercifully the fever passed and it did surprisingly quickly!

Life in London was still wonderful and I gave up on the whole damn dating thing again. Back in Australia for another wonderful summer with my girls gave me time to ponder my next steps in the dating scene. My decision was to give dating another shot when I headed back to

TOP *Relationship masterclass: My girls with their boys –*
Adrian and Emily, Tim and Madeleine.

BOTTOM *The love bear, a gift from Lisa.*

London but to save the heartache I was going to take it a lot more light-heartedly. Changing websites helped put me in contact with more suitable men for my age and demographic. It turned out to be more fun as I would approach each date as if it was just an opportunity to meet someone new and I've put aside any silly notions of meeting Mr Right. Hope springs eternal in affairs of the heart so leaving behind the disastrous 'silver fox' affair, I perused the new website assiduously with much more confidence and experience this time around. A few dates ensued with some carefully chosen and very nice men including a writer and former journalist who I thought I would have something in common with but it didn't really gel, followed by a retired army major who had impeccable manners and a plummy voice. Despite a deliberately provocative comment at dinner where I said I was worried that the dating website 'would be full of Tory old farts', and he replied quickly, 'Well, you are looking at one right now.' There's something in me that has to test any man to see how they will respond. I always have this sense if they can give as good as they get, it may work. I'm simply never going to be a well-behaved, polite Englishwoman. Nope, I am definitely a bolshie Aussie 'pain in the arse'. I seem to lack the man-pleasing gene; maybe because it doesn't come naturally and I feel like I'm being somewhat fake and manipulative.

Undaunted, the retired major at the end of our dinner turned to me and asked, 'How do I figure in the pantheon of your admirers? Would you like to see me again?' I still giggle at the thought of 'a pantheon of admirers'; it seems so wonderfully *Pride and Prejudice*. He kindly invited me to Trooping the Colour, where Her Majesty inspects her splendidly clad Guards, the ones with the big black fur hats. I was thrilled to see the Queen driving around in her carriage in her diamond Jubilee Year. Despite my republican convictions, I feel you have to admire that marvellous woman and her dedication to duty. Not to mention the colour-coordinated ensembles she wears! It was a fascinating day although expensive, as I had to buy a hat and dress. (For those who love

*Pomp and circumstance: Trooping the colour
during the Queen's Diamond Jubilee.*

fashion detail it was an LK Bennett red sheath dress and a little black hat to which I added a big, blowsy red rose.) God, I began to feel like Camilla Parker Bowles. At the smart lunch afterwards at the Guards Club on Piccadilly, I felt like pinching myself – had I dropped into a scene out of *Downton Abbey*? Was this indeed still the 21st century? A wonderful experience but in the end this was not a match made in heaven or anywhere else for that matter.

My life was consumed with writing, lecturing and, after I agreed to go full time at Southampton University in the new term, with the mammoth task of moving from London to the country. The move was to glorious Winchester and a beautiful summer was spent with my daughter Madeleine. After this I was ready again for a foray into the dating world.

So as a reward for meeting the deadline on this book, I decided to go out with someone new who had contacted me online. A classics teacher, who seemed clever and sounded lovely. Our first date, at his suggestion, was seeing an exhibition at the National Gallery. Brownie points for the choice of venue and the choice of exhibition, which had a particular masterpiece by Titian with a classical theme. As I sat on the parapet outside swinging my legs, I felt like a girl watching my date walk across the road towards me. It was a great outing, as interesting as I had imagined, and it blossomed into a grown-up affair. But as quickly as it started it ended.

While I was a bit bewildered for a little while, before long I just accepted that sometimes that's just the way it goes. I found myself being able to roll with the punches a lot more easily than I used to. I'm much more philosophical about it all and if it's not meant to be, it's not meant to be and something else or rather someone else will appear when the time is right. That's the thing about dating: you just never know whether it's going to work or not. Online dating is even more of a gamble but the one thing I have discovered is there is very likely someone else waiting in the wings. It requires a good deal of emotional resilience and a good dose of fatalism. And acceptance of what 'is' rather than resistance to what is happening. The fact that I am now so much happier on my own, something I never would have thought possible in my younger years, makes life all so much easier. As for the notion of Mr Right, I don't believe in the concept any more (maybe I never really did). There are so many people who could be 'right' for you and you just never know when one might appear. I'm all 'right' so no need for a 'Mr Right'!

As for destiny, if it should wing your way you just have to be ready to catch it as it flies by. My new life in Winchester was delightful and my sister Sarah came from Paris to stay for a few days to see my lovely new place. Early on the morning before she was about to go back to Paris we decided to make a visit to the cathedral. It is glorious and as we stood gazing up the beautiful Gothic nave with its soaring stone arches, a well-dressed older man approached with a twinkle in his eye and engaged us in conversation. We chatted about the heavenly architecture and the stained-glass windows; we laughed and even ended up talking about fashion. There was something about him, some instant connection that made me feel like I knew him. I also found this tall, white-haired man indefinably attractive. Now I actually do know him; George and I have been seeing each other for about nine months as I write this. I find him fascinating and infuriating by turns. The gaps in our backgrounds are a constant source of humour or angst depending on the topic. He grew up in working-class Northern England while I grew up in relatively comfortable middle-class Australian suburbia.

One day I commented rather snobbishly on his interior décor, something mean about his rather naff cream leather sofa; his immediate riposte was 'At least my stuff doesn't look like it came out of a skip.' I burst out laughing. In one fell swoop he had consigned my carefully chosen antique treasures to the scrapheap. During the months we have been together there have been many such taste debates. A strong bit of banter and a sense of humour have always been musts on my relationship radar; much more important than any schmaltzy senti-mentality. We have had both rip-roaring arguments and wonderfully fun times. He has driven me all over the countryside because he knows how much I love it, in what he has dubbed 'Driving Miss Daisy'. I must know every country pub in a twenty-mile radius, and no matter that I'm not a drinker, the atmosphere is worth drinking in. And we have been up to London to go to art exhibitions, parties and my favourite shops. It reminds me rather of that fabulous quote by Richard Burton talking about Elizabeth Taylor, 'I introduced her to beer and she introduced me to Bulgari.' Who knows where it will go from here and maybe it can't last but it has been a great time. A relationship is one of those weird and wonderful things in life, an unknowable part of the journey but not the be-all-and-end-all of existence. It can both delight and test you in equal measure. Being happy with yourself in the 'now' is the biggest gift of all. And sometimes, not always, that's exactly how I feel.

*Man for all seasons: George in summer; rose bowers of Mottisfont Abbey,
and in the snow in Winchester 2013.*

WHAT I'VE LEARNT ABOUT

DATING AGAIN

———

I am absolutely NOT any kind of expert on dating and even less on relationships for that matter, but here's what I've learnt. Internet dating requires courage and resilience, and friends to talk to about it. Increasingly it is the way people meet each other. While it was once a hush-hush subject, now there is nothing to be embarrassed about, as it now estimated that one in five people meet online according to figures in the UK.

Do your research and look at all the sites available and choose the one that seems the best for your age group.

When writing your profile, be succinct and funny. Try and be original and personal because after you've waded through many profiles online, the ones that are original and witty really stand out against a morass of clichés. Try and reduce expectations of Mr Right and let go of some of your preconceptions, but also allow yourself to be clear about what you would like from a date. After a few email exchanges don't prolong the connection. Only when you meet up will you get a real sense of the person and know if it has possibilities. Be brave and good luck!

✳

WHAT I'VE LEARNT TO

WEAR ON A DATE

———

I once had to write a story for *Good Housekeeping* as the Fashion Director giving advice to older women on what to wear when starting to date again. The irony was I hadn't been on a date for at least five years. And when I did go it was sort of laughable, as I went into a panic with a clothes blizzard strewn across the room as I tried out my entire wardrobe.

What I do know as a fashion editor is there is a big gulf between wearing what's fashionable and looking good. Looking good is what we are aiming for here. Men, especially older men, generally aren't great followers of fashion. Case in point: their almost universal dislike of Sarah Jessica Parker and her outfits in *Sex and the City*. No wonder Mr Big baulked at the altar; after all, his bride-to-be had a dead bird on her head!

I've had to unlearn my fashion style a bit and just go for looking good. I leave my more outré fashiony pieces in the wardrobe. We don't want to scare the horses! Once before a dinner with a man I went out and bought an inexpensive coral cotton dress with a wrap bodice and gathered skirt, because I felt all my clothes were way too 'fashiony'. My mother thought this was very funny; it was the first time she had seen me buy something cheap to go out in!

Mostly I keep it simple, comfortable and not too try-hard. A pretty and flattering dress in a lovely colour is always a winner. So is something casual such as well-fitting jeans, higher waisted for me to avoid the muffin top, though not naff 'Mom' jeans, as the Americans describe them. Topped with a well-cut jacket and a fitted top it can look subtly alluring and not too try-hard. That and good shiny soft hair, not too much makeup and the best thing of all – a real smile!

*

«

ABOVE
*Seeing the light: On a yoga
retreat in England.*

RIGHT
*In Turkey, happy in the perfect
hot weather clothes: linen kaftan,
Indian leggings and wrap.*

CHAPTER SIX

The Making of
A NEW ME

Yoga, meditation and finding myself

Living in London and not working full time gave me time to get myself into shape mentally, physically and emotionally. Working on particular projects was great because I could concentrate for full-on bursts and then have time to myself. I had time to play in the city I loved, time to travel and most of all it gave me time to work on myself. At the risk of coming over all new age, here are the things that really worked for me.

Developing my yoga practice was a good place to start working. While getting thinner may have been motivated by a desire to start dating again, my yoga has always been driven by a desire for both spiritual and physical wellbeing. My grandmother introduced me to yoga when I was in my teens and ever since then I have dipped in and out of it. At the age of eighty she was still standing on her head every morning. She lived until she was ninety-four. My mother, who is now in her eighties, does yoga and is still very flexible – you'd think she was decades younger. Both women are a testimony to the power of yoga. My younger sister Emma is a dedicated Ashtanga yogini and my sister Martha is a qi gong teacher and near-miraculous cranial sacral therapist (a subtle energy therapy). I am a complete slouch in comparison but I know and have irrefutable evidence from my own family that it works on so many levels.

When I first came to live in London, I found the life centre in Notting Hill and started going regularly to a yoga class given by American Lisa Sanfilippo, who trained in the Anusara method, an American method that emphasises spiritual and physical alignment that I had first discovered in Paris. And so began my regular yoga practice, along with finding a whole new friendship. What a difference one person can make to your life. One day we discovered while chatting after class that we both lived in Belsize Park, literally around the corner from each other. From then on we became fast friends despite a big age gap of twenty-five years (strange but it works). Lisa, an intense New Yorker with an Ivy League education, turned from a serious job at a think-tank to full-time yoga teaching. Lisa is equally at home talking about tantric

TOP
*Yoga en plein air: Lisa teaching her class
(front left) and me (centre right) hoping
to lose a few rolls round the middle.*

LEFT
*In an Armani bikini on the Lido beach,
Venice at 60 years old. Who decreed we
have to wear a one-piece at a certain age?*

Tall poppy: Fields of green in Wiltshire and in Hampshire.

philosophy (no, tantric philosophy is not all about sex) as she is about talking about boys and dating. Needless to say, Lisa has become one of my closest friends in London. And she can really make me laugh. We have become a family away from our own families. We talk almost every day about our lives and loves. We joke about me introducing her to the world of fashion, so much so that now she is sending me email links to pieces she is contemplating buying. One minute we are giggling like a couple of teenage girls or dancing around the room to cheesy pop songs, next minute we are pondering the mysteries of the universe.

What she has done for me is immense; she has helped me change my shape, made me fitter and introduced me to whole new spiritual world of yoga, meditation and chanting, not to mention introducing me to some new and now dear friends. When I moved to Belsize Park I moved my yoga to Triyoga at Primrose Hill where Lisa also taught. Triyoga became one of my favourite places to hang out. I could take yoga class and afterwards eat some healthy vegetarian food in their café and have a natter with Lisa and her friends or have a heavenly hot oil ayurvedic massage from fellow expat Jono Condous. It's a bonus on yoga days that Primrose Hill is so very pretty. I find it lovely to stroll down the main street afterwards to check out the cafés and boutiques. Taking a walk into the park and up to the top of the hill means you can see the panoramic view of London made famous in many a movie. In the recent winter when heavy snow fell in London (a rarity), Primrose Hill was covered in snow and was full of people tobogganing down the hill and children making snowmen. Such a picturesque sight!

It was at Triyoga that I met my friend Susan Watson (the ex-nurse I called on when I had my fainting spell on a London street), the only other person of my age I know who can do an upward-facing bow (a kind of harbour bridge with your body). Susan had come to London to live because she had married her teenage sweetheart after leaving a long marriage and two grown-up sons back in the States – we had quite a bit in common. Lisa, Susan and I started doing things together, having lunch, going to the theatre and on my birthday for the past few years we've gone to some swanky London restaurant to celebrate. I feel so lucky to have made wonderful friends at this stage in my life on the other side of the world.

So yoga has transformed my body and my life in many ways. In my search for wellbeing I have found friends for life. After learning yoga for years I finally managed to do the upward-facing bow or bridge pose on the yoga retreat in Turkey with Lisa and Susan by my side (yes, the same retreat where I met that silver-haired yogi). To suddenly be able to arch up in a wonderful curve seemingly floating in the air was an amazing moment. And it took until I had hit my sixties to be able to do something I never thought I could. It is something that flows through to the rest of my life – never think that anything is impossible.

The other important thing that Lisa introduced me to is the practice of meditation. Through the London meditation centre run by Michael Miller and Jillian Lavender, who teach the ancient tradition of Vedic meditation around the world, I finally found a way to meditate that worked for me. I have often tried to meditate but felt like a failed meditator because I could not hold my mind still. But after training with them I know that is just a matter of sitting for twenty minutes and going back to your mantra every time you drift away – and that drifting off is okay but the key is to acknowledge and refocus. What I've learnt is you cannot force yourself into a meditative state. Give up the struggle, let the thoughts arise and go back again to the mantra and breathing. You just have to keep coming back it. Though I can't say I do it twice a day every day, as is the proper practice, when I do I can feel the difference in my life. And it is not a time-waster; in fact, it makes me more productive in the rest of the day and much calmer.

With all the yoga, Buddhist teachings and meditation I have not turned into some new age 'Pollyanna'. I still get distressed, depressed, angry and just plain sad sometimes for no particular reason. What

Wild flowers on the white cliffs of Sussex.

What we wore: TOP LEFT *Fashion editor
Jane Roarty in vibrant printed silk by
Easton Pearson.* TOP RIGHT *SBS network
stylist Lesley Crawford and designer
Pam Easton in Paris.* LEFT *Juli and me
at the Hermès party on the beach in Sydney
wearing an Hermès scarf and Easton Pearson
dress.* BELOW *Alexandra and me on the
rue Saint-Honoré, Paris.*

has changed is that I now have some tools to help me deal with these shifts. Everyday life continues as it always has, reminding me of the Zen maxim 'before enlightenment chopping wood and carrying water, after enlightenment chopping wood and carrying water'. Make that ironing and vacuuming. As for enlightenment, lord, I have barely scratched the surface.

One of the most profound changes I have had to deal with has nothing to do with moving to the other side of the globe but rather the inexorable process of ageing. Our society does not value age and there is a constant battle especially for a woman to stave off and fight the process. While men seem to be allowed to age naturally in our society, women are somehow meant to stay looking young. Just look at the difference in male and female television presenters as a marker of our society's attitude to age in women. While we women may have been freed from the tyranny of dressing like frumpy matrons and cutting our hair short after a certain age, we are now expected to show no visible signs of ageing. And as far as your face is concerned, you are damned if you do anything to make yourself look younger and damned if you don't.

Working in the fashion media makes me even more acutely aware of the process of ageing and our attitude to it all. When you finally do see a woman over fifty in a magazine, they have usually been so retouched that it's hard to know what 'normal' is these days. The thing I've noticed working in the media is how little we see of any women over forty in the mainstream press. It's as if we don't exist any more. The invisibility cloak is more effective than anything dreamed up by JK Rowling. Whatever publication I've worked for I've tried to counter this and if I have had a speciality in the career I've had, it is to show older women at their best, both famous and not so famous. It is heartening to see that it finally beginning to change as talented, older actresses such as Judi Dench, Helen Mirren, Meryl Streep and Diane Keaton appear in movies as attractive and sexy women, rather than sweet, sad or twisted old ladies.

On a personal level it's a balancing act between acceptance of what is happening and trying to look the best I can. For me the most ageing thing is not your face or your body but your attitude. Well, it's not just your attitude; perhaps it's more what you believe about ageing. Deepak Chopra talks a lot about ageing as an expectation that society has placed on us rather than an inevitable process. Our attitude to ageing is something we can choose and change. We can turn that around by staying involved mentally and active physically. I feel fortunate in the genetic cards I have been dealt but self-loathing has shimmered just below the surface for most of my life as it does in an alarming way for almost all women in our society. So I struggle with ageing and my best way forward. I have also discovered some solutions to these conundrums that are quite achievable.

As I have got older my shoulders have started to hunch over, my back has become rounded and my tummy bulges and the weight has crept up. Yoga has helped me to reshape my body and narrow a thickening torso, though my tummy is stubbornly staying put. When I stop doing yoga, as I have in the past few months because I injured my knee in a stupid slip, the difference is enormous. There's no way around it – we simply have to move. Even if we don't exercise formally, the simple notion of incidental exercise and walking as many steps as we can in a day is vital. One basic thing you can do to look younger is simply to stand up straight and I have to remind myself every day – the old notion of imagining you are pulling a string from the top of your head works for me. This may sound obvious and easy but it's not as straightforward as it sounds. Many people both young and old rest their torso down on their waists, however, as soon as you make a conscious effort to lift your torso from your waist and elongate your body, pulling your navel to your spine (notionally that is), you will instantly look better and younger.

All my life I've eaten like a labourer, which was fine when I was young and skinny. I look at my wedding photos and marvel at how thin I was. Not that I want to be that thin again. I actually do love my curvy figure because after being a skinny-minny it feels so much more womanly, but there are limits and by the time I moved to France I had reached them. That first summer in the south of France I found myself in the beautiful city of Avignon with my sister Sarah, trying on clothes in a very chic boutique. As I came out of the changing room, my darling sister said in a very stern voice, 'Jane, you really should do something about your weight.' Brutal, but it was the wake-up call I needed. Sarah, after years of living in Paris, had fully absorbed the French ethos and we are all aware, after 'that book', that French women do not get fat! Portion control is a big thing in France and they are very strict about not eating between meals. There are even ads on television advising against it. Maybe it's also because so many of them smoke themselves silly. Sarah cycles everywhere in Paris, which keeps her slim and fit. I found just walking everywhere did the trick.

However, maintaining my weight demands constant vigilance. Living in London once I stopped working full time gave me plenty of time for grazing and so it was again time to take myself in hand and dating again as I mentioned before was a motivation. The Dukan diet created by a French doctor was the chosen diet *du jour*. It's all about eating protein and as I'm an inveterate meat-eater, it was perfect for me. Three days of eating virtually only meat and the weight began to drop off me. I kept on it for three months and lost eight kilograms. So it worked, aside from the scary fainting episode detailed in the previous chapter. As Catherine Deneuve says about being older, you have to choose either the 'visage' or the 'derriere' and I chose the face. I noticed that I look too gaunt if I'm thinner than about 62 kilograms so if I can keep below 65, it's all good. For some that would be heffa-lump size but it's about right for me and allows me to eat well. I'm not too obsessive about it and it is the first time I have ever dieted and will probably be the last. It was such a buzz to fit into size 10 clothes again but I'm now back to a size 12 and I'm comfortable with that. The

ABOVE *Summer in Sydney.*

OPPOSITE, TOP *Rustic café in Avignon.*

OPPOSITE, BOTTOM *Cherries.*

effort it takes to stay any smaller is just not worth it. My rules are to eat the best produce you can, organic wherever possible, savour every mouthful, no unconscious eating and, of course, always succumb to the siren call of chocolate.

In this world of plenty it is good to be reminded sometimes of another world where food is so precious. I caught a mini cab (Londoners often order minicabs because they are cheaper than black cabs, pick you up from home and have a set cost for the journey). My driver was a smiley Ethiopian and because I sit in front (I get carsick) I usually chat to the friendly ones. I asked about his national food, always a safe, uncontroversial subject, and he started talking about his childhood. His family ate virtually the same diet every day, mostly a particular grain, which his mother ground each day. Once a month as a special treat, his mother would buy a packet of spaghetti for the whole family. He told me he used to save a tiny bit and drape it on his clothes the next day when he went to school so someone would say, 'What is that on your shirt?' And he would reply, brushing it off casually, 'Oh, that is spaghetti from our dinner.' A strand of spaghetti was a child's status upgrade! He told me that on a really extra special day, when his mother sold a goat, she would buy a packet of chocolate biscuits, which they would ration amongst the family. 'One chocolate biscuit,' he said, 'so much happiness!' Then he came to live in London where there is 'so much chocolate biscuits,' he said, adding, 'little happiness'. I've never seen that man again but his words stay with me.

Being grateful for having so much abundance is one way to find real happiness. If I start losing my way I have to remind myself that I am so incredibly lucky to have the life that I have. The daily practice of gratitude is something I have learned to do. In the book *Happier* by Harvard lecturer Tal Ben-Shahar, where he details the research which found that keeping a daily gratitude journal and writing down five things every night before going to sleep leads to greater emotional and physical wellbeing. The pursuit of happiness has long been enshrined

*What a feeling: Happy, healthy and fit in Turkey
on a yoga retreat with Lisa.*

On the street: Me at London Fashion Week, photographed by
Vanessa Jackman, who photographs at the shows for her blog,
vanessajackman.blogspot.co.uk.

in spiritual thought and it is this central tenet of Buddhist philosophy that resonates with me. As the Dalai Lama says, 'The very purpose of our lives is to seek happiness.' Finding what gives me happiness has been at the heart of my life in the past few years and I can say that this is probably the happiest I have ever been.

One tool I have found incredibly helpful in visualising the life I wanted to lead was creating vision boards. I'd read ages ago a piece by self-help guru Martha Beck in *O, The Oprah Magazine* about preparing a vision board for your life, a kind of scrapbook of images that encapsulate what you want in life. In London I came across a funny piece by writer Viv Groskop in *Red* magazine about her doing such a board and what she came up with. She starts her piece with 'This is the story about a woman who thought she wanted a £2.75 million house, but realised that all she actually needed was a boiled egg.' This intrigued me so much that I decided I was going to give it a go especially as I was feeling that it was time to make a new vision for the future.

So I spent days in my flat in Belsize Park cutting out images from my stash of magazines to create a life map/mood board in pictures. It was a fantastic exercise and it had me thinking about my life and what I wanted to do next. I adored doing the boards – it was like making my own lifestyle pages and my magazine training came to the fore. It really made me review what I wanted for the next stage of my life and helped crystallise my decisions. I talked Lisa into making boards too so we sat around on the floor of my flat surrounded by a sprawling mass of magazines, scissors, glue and mount boards. There was a lot of laughter and even tears along the way as we cut a swathe through the media mountain.

What began as a kind of cosmic shopping list gradually levelled out into things of beauty that give me joy as it shifted from Hermès bags or shiny, coloured jewels, morphing into green fields, dappled sunlit trees, walls of roses, Georgian houses and French windows in country villas. In fact, the pictures turned out to include a whole lot of green and countryside. And here I'd been thinking I had to live right in the centre of a big city!

HOW TO MAKE A VISION BOARD

It's simple really and although it seems slightly nutty and new age, I found it a wonderful experience to focus on what gives me joy. Just cut out things you love no matter how quirky they seem, it can be any little thing that speaks to you. Glueing them down on paper is like doing cosmic decoupage with purpose. Once you've done the boards, love them and then let them do their magic. If you need more guidance, read Martha Beck's piece on the Oprah website.

www.oprah.com/spirit/how-to-make-a-vision-board-find-your-life-ambition-martha-beck/

On the personal front I searched for images of baby boomer women who looked like I'd want to be them (not ads for plus-size frumpiness, incontinence pads or cups of tea), older men (not pension-fund grand-dads but cool, older guys who I actually might find attractive), and older couples who looked delighted to be together (not ersatz couples in retirement village ads). Do you have any idea how hard that is to find? I must have trawled through at least 150 magazines to find little over a few dozen images.

In the end I so loved making my boards that I did four instead of one: one for love, one for life, one for home and one for travel. As I look back on the boards a year later it is actually quite 'spooky' (to quote Dame Edna) as to how many images resemble my life now.

All I can add is whatever appeals, just give it a go. You never know, it might change your life.

ABOVE
Vision boards.

LEFT
*Lisa and me making vision
boards on the kitchen floor.*

EATING WELL

———

My not-negotiable in the live-for-less mode is good food. It is one of life's greatest pleasures. I never stint on good-quality food, but I've learnt to eat at home much more and have a drink in a smart bar as the locals do, for meeting friends, people watching and soaking up the atmosphere. Eating out is so expensive, so that is saved for special times with friends. Buying your own food at the local shops or farmer's market (Marche Biologique in Paris or Marylebone Farmer's market in London) is a wonderful experience. In Paris try Monoprix supermarkets; in London the best supermarket chain is Waitrose (lots of the best organic stuff stocked). I really don't care if it's more expensive. You are what you eat. For ready-made food, go to Marks and Spencer or Pret a Manger for a good salad to go. The food is so much better than some crappy clip joint of a tourist café. If you want a café, Le Pain Quotidien is usually good for a quick brekkie – I love their boiled eggs with French bread. Nothing like a fresh baguette, *jambon et fromage* or a fruit tart from Paul in Paris to gladden your day.

MAKING THE MOST OF
YOUR CROWNING GLORY

———

My friend Maggie Alderson believes in spending her top beauty dollar on good hair – a great cut and colour. Her blonde bob always looks fabulous. She's so right and this is one beauty ritual that can make all the difference. I like to go to Aveda salons to reduce the chemical impact.

DRESSING WELL FOR MY AGE

———

Of course, once you are fit, healthy, standing up straight and walking with ease, then it's about what you wear.

I'm a fashion editor so buying clothes and budgeting is an eternal struggle between desire and debt. What I try to do is buy less, but buy the best I can afford. Sometimes I put a moratorium on myself buying cheap things. I know this may sound counterintuitive but it's a great discipline to stop me spending money. I make this rule as otherwise I can fritter away so much money buying 'affordable' bits that cost little but are a sad compromise, when it could be spent on an investment piece that I would really love.

My fashion mantra is quality, quality, quality! Just like location, location, location in property, the same rule applies. When it comes to fashion, my favourite theory is 'cost per wear'. Something cheap may cost you $15 but if you never wear it, you've thrown your money away. You might as well rip up dollar bills. Something that costs $250 may be expensive at the time but if you wear it for ten years, the cost per wear amortises to very little. It's a marvellous rationalisation for buying something very expensive. Buying trousers or jeans is such a nightmare that when I find the right cut, I don't quibble about the price. I had a pair of Ralph Lauren black fine wool trousers for a decade and wore them every winter; as I live in England that's virtually eight months a year. I had to give them away when the fabric on the inner thigh became transparent!

Dressing for your age has never been trickier. We are able to dress so much younger than our mother's generation; in fact mothers and daughters can often wear the same thing but navigating what works for us is not so easy. Young girls may be able to wear cheap disposable fashion, older women just can't. We don't want to look like mutton dressed as lamb, but nor do we want to be damned into some eternal mother-of-the-bride scenario. So what to do?

>

What works for me are chic well-tailored clothes, classics with a modern fashion mood and feel-good luxury. Great jackets and clever coats are my go-to wardrobe staples from labels like Martin Grant, Paul Smith, Gerard Darel and Diane von Furstenberg (most gleaned from winter sales). For summer I go a bit floatier with fine linens, a pretty dress or a bit of a breakout into boho brilliance from a label like Easton Pearson.

For years I've worn a lot of fashionista black and it still is my staple, forming the base of my whole wardrobe. It's saved my fashion bacon many a time. Stylists Trinny and Susannah did go on a lot about not wearing black because it's 'ageing' but I don't agree. I find chic, quality black clothes last for years and always look good. However, colour has really emerged again in the fashion lexicon, so I've made a conscious effort to introduce much more into my wardrobe especially after a recent boyfriend asked why I wore so much black.

Trinny and Susannah were so right about one thing – wear more fitted clothes. One tends, when bigger, to wear things bigger, which in turn makes one look . . . bigger. Fitted, that is, not tight, unless we are talking stretch jeans, which slide down and bag unless they are really fitted. I took my friend Loene into a London department store to buy some 'Not Your Daughter's Jeans', that great American brand of stretch jeans that claim to make you one size smaller. I kept making her try a size smaller, she kept protesting; finally they were tight and she looked terrific and didn't want to take them off.

＊

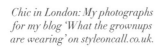

*Chic in London: My photographs
for my blog 'What the grownups
are wearing' on styleoncall.co.uk.*

CLOCKWISE FROM TOP LEFT
*Hotelier Kit Kemp at her interiors
book launch at the Soho hotel;
creative director of British Vogue
Lucinda Chambers at London
Fashion Week; legendary retailer
'Mrs B' of Browns (Joan Burstein)
at a Christopher Kane show;
fashion director Paula Reid at
the London launch of the
International Woolmark prize;
retailer Ruth Chapman of
matches.com*

BEAUTY AT A CERTAIN AGE

If I have one mentor on how to age well, cliché though it may be, it is Audrey Hepburn. She aged with such grace and dignity and in her last years the images of her as UNICEF ambassador show her divine, serene beauty.

Our society is so hell bent on women not ageing that we have almost forgotten how it looks to grow old gracefully. I have no particular moral objection to either plastic surgery or cosmetic procedures. I just think most people look worse afterwards. Whole swathes of women around the world are starting to look like alien sisters with puffed-up lips, odd monkey-like protuberances above the upper lip and strangely pulled-up eyes. There must be a better way to look good.

✳

SKINCARE

———

So where do I go to get advice on how to look good? I always love reading what other women use, so perhaps you'd like to read my list. I have super sensitive skin so I can't use many of the whizz-bang products with very active ingredients that would help 'mature' skins. As I don't work on a magazine that is desperate to please advertisers, I'll mention the products I actually use. I find *The Anti Ageing Beauty Bible* by Josephine Fairley and Sarah Stacey very useful as they have editorial independence and have a whole volunteer army of testers. Check out their website too: www.beautybible.com

I find the scent of roses very calming and nurturing and for this reason I have used Ren the British skincare brand for years, particularly any of their Moroccan rose products, such as the body and bath oils. I'm also using their Radiance and the Sensitive skincare ranges, and my must-have product is their cleansing beauty balm, Ren No. 1 Purity Cleansing Balm, which comes in a plastic tube and is the most soothing makeup remover I've used. I wash it off with a hot, wet face washer and my face feels soft and soothed afterwards. I love Ren's small packs of sample size tubes, which are great for travelling. See their website www.renskincare.com

For a home-grown Australian brand, created in South Australia, I love Janesce, particularly their Softening Wonder cream. It is a divine moisturiser that smells of roses and I also use their beautiful rose facial drops.

Aside from the natural beauty of Ren and Janesce, I am also playing with the rose-scented luxury beauty products of the French skincare brand By Terry, especially her Creme de Rose. Her products are available from Space NK in London and Mecca Cosmetica in Sydney.

✳

WHAT I'VE LEARNT ABOUT

UPDATING MY MAKEUP

———

One of the best ways to look good is by simply updating your makeup look. Many women get stuck like a fly stuck in amber, with their Groundhog Day makeup from a time when they felt they looked their best. So I go to the makeup counter and find an older woman who looks good and ask her to try some new products on me. I find the Bobbi Brown counter very helpful. I also love visiting Mecca Cosmetica in Sydney or Space NK in London to browse cult beauty from around the world, get advice and try products.

I follow the 'less is more' maxim, as the older you get the less makeup you should be wearing. But that doesn't necessarily mean no makeup, it means artfully applied 'no makeup'. I watch the videos online of English celebrity makeup artist Lisa Eldridge, which I find excellent and her 'no makeup' and long-haul flight videos are instructive and entertaining.

Foundation is all-important; something sheer and with some SPF in it as I seem to be allergic to most SPF products on their own. (They make my face peel and irritate my eyes.) At the moment I'm loving Chantecaille's Just Skin with SPF 15 as it comes in a tube useful for travelling, and at home and in the evening I'm using Yves Saint Laurent Le Teint Touch Eclat. Armani's Face Fabric with SPF 12 also comes in a tube. I like to mix it up depending on whether is day or night, and according to the seasons.

The most important thing you can own as you get older is a magnifying mirror. Very scary when you first look in it but, hey, you get used to it. Great for plucking, it can also be vital for putting on eye makeup without your reading glasses. I use a long-lasting gel eyeliner and it's tricky to apply so I could not do it without my magnifying mirror; 10X magnification is the best.

As I like a liquid eyeliner with a bit of cat's eye flick, I swear by Bobbi Brown Long-wear Gel Eyeliner: with my super-sensitive eyes this is the only one I can use and it really does last all day. Keep the lid on tight as it dries out easily. It is tricky to apply and takes lots of practice. I find their brush useless and use a great one by Shu Uemura with a cap that sticks on the end so you never lose it. I use everyday MAC Browset, which is a clear eyebrow gel that keeps unruly brows groomed all day. It makes a difference if you haven't tried it before.

As for lipsticks, I have so many as it is my little affordable luxury. MAC still makes the best lipsticks and has the best colours. My current faves are pretty corals, 'Vegas Volt' and 'Ravishing', bright orange 'Morange' and browny beiges 'Freckle Tone' and 'Stay in Touch'. I'm also loving the new Bobbi Brown mattes that don't bleed into the lines around your mouth. I use a lip primer such as MAC prep and prime to hold the lipstick

I avoid shimmer in all products as I think it looks bad on older skin. Looking in the mirror and finding nasty little bits of sparkle all around the lines in your mouth or around your eyes is just horrid. I avoid powders as it settles in the creases and it tends to age you. I think cream products are softer and dewier on older skin, so I use cream blusher rather than powder in a subtle pinky coral from Bobbi Brown.

✳

THE LISTING
WELLBEING IN LONDON

———

THE HODGE CENTRE

www.thehodgecentre.com

For wonderful gentle energy work make an appointment with yoga practitioner Vanessa Hodge for a cranial-sacral treatment.

THE LIFE CENTRE

www.thelifecentre.com/nottinghill
15 Edge Street,
Notting Hill, London W8 7PN
Telephone: + 44 (0) 20 7221 4602

One of the original London yoga centres that provides yoga classes and therapies of different styles. There is also a centre now opened in Islington.
  Look out for Kirtan chanting evenings at the Life Centre with devotional singer Narayani and see her website for other events and her music: **www.onebodyonesound.com**

LISA SANFILIPPO YOGA

www.lisayogalondon.com

My friend and yoga teacher Lisa gives fantastic classes at both Triyoga and The Life Centre. She also teaches privately and holds wonderful workshops in England, France, Italy and Asia. Check out her website for upcoming yoga retreats.

LONDON MEDITATION CENTRE

www.londonmeditationcentre.com

Meditation taught by Michael Miller and Jillian Lavender, from the ancient Vedic meditation tradition. Once you have done the course you can attend one of the group meditation courses held in Notting Hill. It is a powerful thing to sit in a room with a few hundred other people meditating.

TRIYOGA

www.triyoga.co.uk
6 Erskine road
Primrose Hill, London NW3 3AJ
Telephone: +44 (0) 20 7483 3344

At Triyoga (also in Chelsea and Soho) one can do many styles of yoga or choose from an incredible range of amazing therapies and beauty treatments. (So good for jetlag!) My favourite is a hot oil Ayurvedic massage from Jono Condous. Afterwards, take a moment in the café to have a fresh juice or eat healthy veggie food around a communal table.

WELLBEING IN SYDNEY

———

IN GOOD HANDS MASSAGE THERAPY

**www.naturaltherapypages.com.au/
connect/ingoodhands/service/2017
340 Clovelly Road
Clovelly NSW 2031**

To restore me to some sort of working order after a long-haul flight, I head down to this sweet little shop not far from the beach where Tania Griffin and Lizzie Milligan give excellent remedial massages. This is not some prissy, feathery beauty salon massage but the real thing – strong and powerful. When Tania works on my body resting on a mattress on the floor I can feel the kinks unravelling. Since I have been away, my sister Martha Regnault has begun coming to Sydney once a month to do a day of cranial-sacral treatments at In Good Hands. I'm not biased – these treatments are nothing short of miraculous in the subtlest possible way.

YOGA SYNERGY

**115 Bronte Road,
Bondi Junction, NSW 2022
Telephone: +61 (02) 9389 7399**

When I began my return to yoga, this is where I came to learn at one of Sydney's most respected yoga schools.

BOOKS I TURN TO

———

Ageless Body Timeless Mind and
The Seven Spiritual Laws of Success
by Deepak Chopra

*The Power of Now: A guide to spiritual
enlightenment* by Eckhart Tolle

*Mindfulness: A practical guide to finding
peace in a frantic world* by Mark Williams
and Danny Perlman

Happier by Tal Ben-Shahar

And for something completely different – clever wonderful women writers who make me laugh:

The Pursuit of Love by Nancy Mitford

*I Feel Bad About My Neck: And
other thoughts on being a woman*
by Nora Ephron

How to Be a Woman by Caitlin Moran

THIS PAGE
Mountain high: The rooftops of the village in the Cevennes, where my sister Sarah and family have their stone house.

RIGHT
Summer Sydney: Me at a Hermès party on the beach.

CHAPTER SEVEN

'Everywhere you go
THERE YOU ARE'

VIA AIR MAIL

A restless spirit

If you were to ask me what my absolute favourite pastime is, my answer would be travelling. There is nothing I love more than the anticipation of catching a train or plane and going somewhere else. I know for some that longed-for destination is some chic designer resort, where one can lie around a turquoise pool, reading books, eating Michelin-star food and quaffing wine – it all sounds great but nope, it's not my kind of travel. For me a holiday is a time to discover everything about a place from the most glam hotel down to the minutiae of the local supermarket. Exploring the streets or the countryside, people watching, going to the local markets; I always want to be a part of the life around me. Even better is when my destination has a purpose. Going where I have a purpose and the place has a purpose, such as Venice during the Biennale, Arles during Les Rencontres d'Arles or Edinburgh during the Festival. That's my ideal holiday, fascinating things to see and do in a beautiful place.

When I first came to Paris to live, it was the south of France that I had a burning desire to explore, especially as my sister had a place there. The baking climate and the harshness of the landscape have a feeling of home with the exotic flavour of a French culture which is wilder and less manicured than Paris. As you step out of the railway station in Nimes, the heat hits you smack in the face and you're immediately immersed in ancient Roman France. The beautiful Roman temple dominates the main square and close by is the amazingly preserved massive Roman amphitheatre, which is still used for everything from bullfights to pop concerts. Madeleine and I went there with Sarah and her husband Robert to see an amazing concert by Björk who, from up in the gods area of the arena, appeared to be a tiny, mad, dancing fairy in a rainbow-coloured dress.

As an aside, did you know that that the word 'denim' comes from *de Nimes* (from Nimes), a durable indigo-dyed cotton cloth, imported to the gold fields of California in the 19th century? That working man's cloth has gone on to become part of the most ubiquitous fashion item in the world.

TOP LEFT *Travelling: Me in Paris in favourite
panama hat and long pink shirt dress.*
TOP RIGHT *Marseille through hotel window.*
ABOVE LEFT *Edinburgh during the fringe
festival.* ABOVE RIGHT *Me in Marrakech
on a shoot.*

Cévennes scenes: CLOCKWISE FROM RIGHT *Horsemen in the village of Breau, bicyclist after a summer storm, south of France, rooftop in the haze.*

'EVERYWHERE YOU GO, THERE YOU ARE.'

Not far from Nimes are the Cevennes Mountains and National Park. There is something wild and wonderful about the Cevennes that strips away the trappings of urban life into an ancient and elemental simplicity. During that first summer when I moved to France, Mads and I stayed down in a charming stone house just a step across from Sarah's 'stone tent'. We often walked five kilometres from her village down through the forest to the next tiny village called Breau, the coloured stripes on trees guiding us on the right paths. These stripes have been painted for the *randonneurs*, who hike through France on an intricate network of walks. Sometimes you come across them, replete with poles, backpacks and huge plastic labels around their necks, which make them look like geriatric pre-schoolers on an excursion. Writer Robert Louis Stevenson took a donkey trek in the middle of the 19th century across the Cevennes and, in a way, very little has changed; if he were alive he would still recognise the raw landscape he traversed. You can, if you are adventurous and into serious walking, still take a donkey trek across the mountains. An intriguing notion but not my idea of comfort!

After the relative wilds of the Cevennes, I felt a longing to visit some pretty Provençal towns. Madeleine and I set out on our own in a mother/daughter bonding road trip, much like the ones we used to take when they were younger (just me and the girls singing at the top of our lungs driving through the Australian outback). I hired a tiny car in Nimes and attempted to drive a manual again (most French hire cars are manuals) and on the 'wrong' side of the road. My efforts down the tiny country roads of France had Madeleine shouting in horror (eventually we settled on a system of batlike squeaks she was allowed to emit when I got too close to the kerb or strayed on the wrong side of the road). We left the tiny village of Esparon perched on its eagle's nest and drove further east to another 'Esparron' or Esparron-de-Verdon (it piqued my interest, the names being so similar) in the Provence-Alpes-Côte d'Azur region in south-eastern France, where I booked us a few nights at Château d'Esparron, which I had read about in a travel magazine and filed away for some longed-for future in Europe. Not too grand, the château is charming with the unpretentious air of an ancient family home. Worn flagstones, comfy bedrooms perched up high, overlooking the garden and fresh sunflowers on the kitchen windowsill (picked from the garden), it was a lovely place for the two of us to spend time together. It was so hot that we hired a ridiculous pedal boat on a weirdly blue man-made lake nearby and plunged into the heart-stoppingly cold depths. It's always a buzz diving into deep water without worrying about any sharp-toothed killers lurking below the surface, a sly fear imprinted on Australian brains.

We then drove to the picture-postcard-pretty town of Saint-Rémy-de-Provence and browsed the chic boutiques, testing Madeleine's tolerance of shopping to the limits of her patience. We visited the charming Provençal village of Eygaliéres where I wanted to stay forever and did some sightseeing at the hill top town Les Baux, which is just a tad Disneyland touristy, though the landscape is spectacular. We picnicked on delicious rotisserie chicken, that French speciality, in an idyllic setting complete with antique statuary looking up at Les Baux. Madeleine still reminds me to this day about my folly in throwing a chicken bone to a buzzing wasp to distract it, only to be rewarded by an entire swarm descending and driving us out of said romantic idyll.

In a bid to find more stimulating cultural material for the soul rather than a thousand cuts by lavender bag of the tourist shops, I planned a trip to Arles as part of our itinerary to-ing and fro-ing across Provence. I'd read about the fantastic photography festival, *Les Rencontres d'Arles Photographie*. It is a marvellously curated series of international exhibitions, held all over the town from the windswept disused railway yards to crumbling chapels.

Arles is a mysterious city with a somewhat dark soul. With an ancient burial ground, Les Alyscamps, which goes back to Roman times as does the arena where bullfighting is still held, Arles is an intriguing

French vignettes: LEFT *Brocante near Le Vigan.*
BELOW *Pink flower and cobbles of Esparon.*
BOTTOM LEFT *The pink anchovy house in Collioure.*
BOTTOM RIGHT *Les Alyscamps in Arles.*

'EVERYWHERE
YOU GO, THERE
YOU ARE.'

210

French country stays: CLOCKWISE FROM TOP
Hot and hazy white horse; cobbled village stairs; Sanglier Lodge,
a divine B&B in Le Tech in the French Pyrénées;
Café at Auberge des Quatre Saisons, Breau, France.

mix of centuries of history from Roman to early Christian and beyond. The Romanesque church in the main square, Saint Trophime, is a cool, grey respite of calm and order, in the midst of all the heat and craziness. Behind the church there's an ancient medieval cloister with beautiful life-size saints carved into the columns – simply miraculous.

The hot wind, which blows across the city in summer, scorching everything in its wake, adds to the strange unsettled air of Arles. No wonder it was the place where Vincent Van Gogh came to paint, lured by the intense light and colour. In the space of a year, with the crazy energy generated, undoubtedly from his own madness and the swirling force-field within the town, he produced more than 200 canvases including the famous yellow *Café at Night*. That café no longer exists but a reproduction of it sits in the main square. While I would have liked to stay in the Grand Hotel Nord-Pinus, where Hemingway, Picasso and Cocteau used to hang out with the bullfighters, I was perfectly content with a drink in the atmospheric bullfighters bar while we stayed in a very simple hotel nearby, of a sparse backpackers standard (sadly since disappeared).

Each year since that first visit I've made a pilgrimage to Arles at festival time. My photographer friend Juli Balla and I visited one year and as a bit of a splurge booked into Château de Roussan, a pretty hotel just near Saint Rémy de Provence. We dined *al fresco* on the terrace on a hot evening with the sounds of the burbling river and smells of the countryside surrounding us. We drove into Arles (about thirty minutes away) each day and exhausted ourselves exploring the exhibitions (including a confronting one by Nan Goldin about her life that still sticks in my mind) then took leave of the frenetic town and came back to the cool calm of the chateau. Heaven.

A Provençal town that I always find magical is Aix en Provence, so beautiful with the soulful attraction of it being the town where Cezanne was born, lived and died. Madeleine and I made a pilgrimage out of the town and up the hill by bus to Cezanne's last studio. Artist studios and houses are such evocative places and Cezanne's studio is absolutely charming. Although there's not a Cezanne painting to be found, the sight of the beautiful studio with old coats still hanging in the corner and many of the objects he used in his paintings lined up along a shelf is deeply affecting. If I could have moved in I would have. I begged the girl on the door to let me take some photographs, although they are forbidden, and she allowed me to sneak back after the tour had gone and do just that. It was the highlight of that trip, where the dust of centuries fell away and I could see the life and work of Cezanne come to life. Afterwards it was worth the breathless struggle up the steep hill that he would have walked up to take in the breathtaking view of his favourite subject, Mont Sainte Victoire, with its dark green pines, orange roofs and chalky planes of raw rock at the peak.

Everywhere in Aix one finds beauty, from the crumbling *hôtels particuliers* (grand townhouses) to the lovely markets in the Square des Prêcheurs. It's a place I love to return to, coming back several times once I had moved to London. On one trip I stayed with my foodie friend, Sarah Canet, in a villa out in the countryside. We motored into the city in her hilarious Deux Cheveaux, that cartoonish little French car, to do the food shopping at the markets where I was serenaded, with my vegetable box held aloft, by a street jazz band. And the shopping in Aix (without my beloved long-suffering daughter Madeleine) is *très* chic with affordable and luxury designer stores, along with Gago, Aix's top multibrand boutique, which tops my shopping/nose pressed against the window list.

On our first trip Madeleine finally said she had had enough of the charming plane-tree-lined squares of Provence, and urged me to take a risk and go down to the coast to visit Marseille. The raffish down-at-heel port had the slightly sinister undercurrent that all rough-and-tumble seaports seem to have, and lived up to my prejudices. And yet Madeleine adored it. We stayed in a bizarre rainbow-hued hotel with peeling wallpapers that looked like something out of a B-grade

Art pilgrimage: CLOCKWISE FROM TOP *Cezanne's studio in Aix en Provence.*
Château de Roussan where Juli and I stayed in St-Rémy-de-Provence during
the photographic exhibition in Arles. Countryside tower.

Mediterrean scene: The Calanques outside Marseille.

crime novel. Our room looked straight out to sea and my photograph of Mads framed by the French doors of this seedy hotel is still one of my favourites.

The chalky white cliffs of the *calanques*, towering over brilliant blue sea, are as marvellous as the paintings of them done by many post-Impressionist painters and we hiked across the rocks for what seemed like ages, until we came to the restaurant I have read about called La Baie des Singes. It was a simple whitewashed building by the sea that's more down-at-heel bathing pavilion than smart restaurant. We were served a terrific meal of fresh fish as we sat outside, watching boats go by while the stiff sea breezes cooled our sunburnt brows.

The next time I returned to Marseille, it was for my architect brother-in-law Robert's birthday. That's the beauty of living in London, Europe is just a cheap flight away and perfect for a long weekend away. He'd organised a group of us to stay in Hôtel Le Corbusier in the important modernist masterpiece, Unité d'Habitation, a block of 350 flats built in the late 1940s out in the suburbs. The rooms and the furniture appeared very much as they would have when it was first built in the early 1950s. It was slightly shabby and thus super-cool. Staying there was an experience so authentic that I felt like I'd dropped into *Monsieur Hulot's Holiday*. And Robert's birthday dinner was held in the very apt restaurant le Ventre de L'Architecte (Belly of an Architect), with a small group of family and friends from Paris and London. We took a fascinating tour of one of the apartments in the building and saw an original kitchen designed by Charlotte Perriand, all clever modernist chutes and metallic finishes, now worn from decades of use.

We hiked for miles across the *calanques* and climbed down into a tiny beach crawling with French sunbathers. Robert surprised us all when a boat arrived to pick us up from the beach. Along the white cliffs we cruised, stopping along the way to dive into the clear blue sea and explore an underwater cave. It was magic to have my nephews and sister diving around me like happy seals.

There is something about water and a breeze off the sea that always makes me happy, having grown up on the coast of Australia all my life. The siren call of Venice has always beckoned as far back as primary school when I was told there was a city in the world that had water canals for roads. I remember thinking such a place must only exist in fairy tales and if it did truly exist, I wanted to see it for myself. *Death in Venice* set on the Venetian Lido with Dirk Bogarde hankering after a beauteous Polish boy, dying as the hair dye ran down his face, cemented my longing. As did the scary but beautiful *Don't Look Now* with a grieving Julie Christie and Donald Sutherland haunted by a red-cloaked gnome disappearing along the canals. On my first trip to Venice in the 1970s, the city was the closest thing to a fairy tale I'd ever seen.

I've made the pilgrimage every two years from London to visit the city romantically known as La Serenissima, during the Biennale. For the decades since I was junior curator I had heard talk of the Venice Biennale, the foremost contemporary art exhibition, which has been going for more than a century (every two years, in odd-numbered years). And at last I managed to get there in a year that the Biennale was being held and it was mind-blowing. It was a chilly November and the city had been emptied of the usual masses of tourists. All over Venice there are Biennale exhibitions and installations; it's such a fantastic way to see the city and see contemporary art in the most incredible locations. The main pavilions are at the Giardini della Biennale, built over a century ago by Napoleon Bonaparte, who drained an area of marshland to create a park within promenading distance from St Mark's Square and the Doge's Palace. Over the century, the pavilions have been built by participating countries with a legacy that is a strange mix of styles and periods. The exhibitions sprawl out into the huge old shipyard buildings at the Arsenale. The Giardini and Arsenale are just the starting point, as the whole of Venice is threaded throughout with Biennale art in the alleyways and canals, in sundry ornate palazzos, in crumbling basements on the canals and in grand churches. For my first Biennale experience I went with contemporary art lover Juli Balla. We stayed in a quaint hotel Casa Martini and caught the vaporettos that ferry the Venetians along the breathtaking canals. It was atmospherically cold and the *aqua alta* (high water), at the time, was seeping out of the canals and across the footpaths and right across St Mark's Square. Each evening to help us warm up we sat in the ornate gilded salon of the famous Café Florian and sipped thick hot chocolate, while people-watching and taking photographs of each other in the sumptuous surrounds. We watched with fascination at the unfolding engagement tableau of a young Russian couple. He had taken one of the private salons in the Florian, engaged a chamber orchestra to play and hired an actor to dress up as a very convincing Renaissance Doge of Venice complete with costumed retinue to greet his intended, who was dressed in a sparkly pink T-shirt, hotpants and trainers, and I watched the whole bizarre scenario from our seats as it played out. By the time we left the Café Florian, a cloud-shrouded moon was rising above the pink and white filigree arches of the Doge's Palace. We felt as though we had been caught in a wonderland.

On one of our many vaporetto hops we stopped off at the magnificent Customs House with the giant gold globe atop, to visit the new contemporary art museum Alla Punta delle Dogana, set up by François Pinault, the French luxury goods mega magnate. On a Sunday we waded through the water lapping over the edge of the canal to Da Marisa to a tiny restaurant by the canal. I'd begged for a booking, any booking, during our stay and managed to get a spot for Sunday lunch. I'd been once before a long time ago on a balmy summer night for my artist friend Loene's birthday and it was so good I vowed to come back again. This time Juli and I crammed ourselves in between local Italians who were packed like sardines into the tiny dining room, as a tempest raged outside. There is no menu, it simply comes as the cook chooses; course after course of fresh fish and the best seafood lasagne I've ever eaten. (Damn, now I've told you I may have to kill you!)

789

'EVERYWHERE
YOU GO, THERE
YOU ARE.'

218

Venetian fairytale:

TOP *Me canalside.*
Photo: Loene Furler

RIGHT *The wonderful Fortuny
Museum during the Biennale.*

OPPOSITE *On the grand canal.*

If I were to name one place that conjures up the magic of Venice, it would be the Palazzo Fortuny, once the home of the genius designer Mariano Fortuny, who designed rich neo-renaissance textiles, fluted Grecian-inspired silk dresses and even huge industrial lamps. During the Biennale, this crumbling palazzo is the venue for the most beautifully curated shows of art I have seen. It is an exquisite mix of ancient and modern pieces in a dream setting and it is all put together by Belgian collector, Axel Vervoordt.

The next time I went to Venice, Loene and I stayed with her friends Sarah and Francesco who live over on the Lido (close to the Edwardian-striped pavilions on the beach in *Death in Venice*). It was summer and meltingly hot. It was also the time of the Biennale and the Venice Film Festival and we were spoilt for choice. In the evenings we bought tickets to the film festival screenings, during the day we went to the Biennale and in between we drank spritzers – the cooling Campari sodas loved by the locals. We went to the beach and walked along the wilder fringes of the Lido where they have built a clandestine hut out of driftwood. I felt like an actress in an Italian art house movie.

The feeling intensified as a day later I headed off to meet my silver-haired paramour, who came from London to spend a weekend with me in Venice. How impossibly romantic to be waiting nervously by the Canal at the vaporetto stop in the dazzling sun as he stepped off the ferry like an old-time movie star to meet me. We stayed in a little pensione, which amused him, as he appeared to never to have stayed in anything so modest before. Simple it may have been, but our room did have a soaring frescoed ceiling. I took him to the Biennale and we wandered through the pavilions, which alternatively shocked or intrigued him. We walked the streets, hand in hand, as he broke into song and I swear he skipped along, we laughed, we sat on a park bench in the shade, we had aperitifs and *cicchetti* (Venetian tapas) in a tiny bar we found one evening and it was a wonderful, romantic dream. And like all dreams, it came to an end. All in all it's a bittersweet memory that is perfectly

TOP *Magic: Venetian Francesco rowing Loene and me in a traditional Venetian rowboat from the Lido to the grand canal.*

BOTTOM *Streetside Madonna.*

Mallorca learning:

TOP *A view of Mallorca, taken on the photography course.*

ABOVE RIGHT *Pollenca cat in hilltop church.*

LEFT *Me on the balcony by fellow student Donna.*

in tune with the somewhat melancholy mood of Venice. As time passes it seems like some cinematic interlude that happened to someone else.

Ah, romance . . . be damned. Travelling on your own can also be great and that's where the purpose becomes all-important. I read travel magazines and squirrel away articles that interest me. One piece piqued my interest, describing one woman's trip to attend a photographic workshop. What did we do before the Internet? The website for eyephotography.com looked very smart, the venue looked divine and the photographer much praised for his patience (he'd need it dealing with me and my inability to concentrate on numbers and figures for more than a few minutes). It sounded like a wonderful chance to combine travel with my growing passion for taking photographs. It sounded right down my alley, learning photography in a beautiful location. So off I went to Mallorca (also known as Majorca), an island off the coast of Spain, somewhere I had never been. As luck would have it the group shrank to just two students – a lovely English woman named Donna, and me. We had a terrific time with photographer/teacher Michael Potter, who was as patient as described. The house in Pollença (a town in the far north corner of the island) was a beautiful old two-storey villa built around a courtyard in the Spanish style, with beautiful shutters and 'French' windows. Wandering around the old city, climbing up to a monastery on the hill above and, one day, when it was raining, turning the camera on each other, was really fun. And I actually learnt something, coming away from the workshop with some lovely images. After years of working with photographers and creating images with them I now wanted to be able to do it myself. The advent of digital photography has made this so much more accessible. How I wish I had paid more attention to what all those photographers were doing. Now it's a constant learning curve and taking photographs while travelling is a source of fascination for me nowadays.

When friend and painter Loene Furler had works included in an exhibition of Australian art held in the Basque town of San Sebastian, we flew to meet up there, me from London, she from Adelaide. After the opening, we made a pilgrimage by car across the mountains to the extraordinary contemporary art museum Guggenheim, designed by Frank Gehry. This is the place for high-impact art and architecture on a powerful scale, with Jeff Koons' giant kitsch *Puppy* in bloom, standing guard at the entrance and Louise Bourgeois' sinister spider sculpture *Maman* flanking riverside of the metal clad art museum. When we were in Venice we loved visiting eccentric art patron Peggy Guggenheim's Palazzo on the canal, once owned by the equally eccentric art patron and artist's muse Marchesa Casati.

'England, my England.' To me there is nothing more beautiful than an English summer in the countryside – that is when it's not raining. When the sun shines on a myriad palette of greens and fluffy white clouds scud gently across a blue sky, I'm in heaven. Once I came to live in England I wanted to go farther afield than London, which seems to hold you in its alluring folds and never lets you stray. But once the summer comes the bonds are loosed and the country calls.

My English friend Susan Millard and I became friends from the day she took me, the new *Good Housekeeping* Fashion Director, to afternoon tea at The Wolseley, the grand café on Piccadilly. We discovered we lived in the same mansion block in Maida Vale and we became pals from that point. One summer she invited me down to stay in a little cottage in Cornwall in a tiny village called Treen that is perched on the cliff tops. We took the train from London to Penzance and it took six hours to the westernmost tip of the English coast. The English, despite having invented train travel, have failed miserably to live up to the modern era, unlike the French whose fast trains can whisk you the same distance in half the time. When I complained to a rail official about the dismally old-fashioned, expensive and over-complicated

Flower madness: Jeff Koons' Puppy *in front of the fantastic Guggenheim in Bilbao.*

TOP *Cornwall blue: The Abbey hotel in Penzance, owned by Jean Shrimpton.*
BOTTOM *Fishing village, Cornwall.*

system, he drew himself up to his full height and said with great dignity, 'Don't blame me, Madam, blame Margaret Thatcher.'

Arriving in Treen was like skipping a century or two as it was a place so peaceful and empty, surrounded by green fields that ran to the rugged cliffs. In the morning, one just ducked down the road for fresh milk straight from the cows at the dairy or bought fresh fruit from a farm table and placed money in an honesty box. In the evening, it was a cider and dinner in the local pub called the Logan Rock Inn. We bought bus passes for a whole £12 each that took us all over the region for days. The tourist bus was an hilarious open-top double-decker with bilious purple seats. Sitting upstairs, the sun on our faces and the wind in our hair, we wound our way through villages and along coastlines – it was the best fun. Sometimes budget travel is way more fun. Those experiences often stick in my mind while the grander ones disappear.

In Penzance we walked around the town, down to the pretty blue neo-Gothic abbey, owned by my teenage heroine the beautiful Jean Shrimpton. I was thrilled when I caught a glimpse of a tall, slim, older woman walking towards the hotel. I just knew it was her and as I drew level to the front door she turned and smiled so sweetly at me and I could see in the fine features, lined gently with age, the face that captivated me so many years ago. I smiled back, too shy to say anything.

At St Ives we walked along the beach in front of the Tate Gallery, then visited the works of art that had been created there. St Ives has long been the town many artists love to work in and many 20th-century British artists are associated with it. Another day we caught the funny purple bus again and visit the most picturesque village around called charmingly Mousehole, pronounced 'Mowzel'. We stayed on for dinner in an open-air courtyard and when we emerged from the restaurant, the village resembled an opera set with a deep blue sky, the moon peeking out from behind a cloud and a man singing an aria beside the fishing port that had been strung with coloured lights. Adorable.

One summer, after I had been living in London for a few years,

I toured some of England's loveliest gardens with my mother Rae, who had come to England particularly for the Victoria and Albert quilt exhibition. We went with her dear friends David and Sebastian, who were also in the country, to view some English gardens in the Cotswolds and in Gloucestershire. An unusual quartet, we wended our way through the Cotswolds countryside seeing some breathtaking gardens on glorious summer days. From the formal gardens of Hidcote Manor, the wonderful rose bowers of private garden Kiftsgate created by three generations of women gardeners, then to Sezincote, an extraordinary Mughal folly built in 1810 in the midst of the Gloucestershire fields. Over the days we experienced the glory of the English garden in beautiful weather. Maybe one day when I'm a real grown-up I'll become a gardener!

A foray to Edinburgh, the capital of Scotland for a few days, is a wonderful thing to do. I found myself there with my daughter Mads, who came to stay with me when I first moved to Winchester (more about that in chapter eight). We flew from nearby Southampton airport to Edinburgh to watch her friend Claudia O' Doherty, an Australian comedian, perform in the Edinburgh Festival Fringe. We booked a quaint little Georgian apartment right on the Royal Mile, through the clever website Airbnb, that lets you book to stay in private house and apartments. We were right in the middle of it all, with a helluva lot of tipsy twenty- and thirty-somethings coursing through the streets, all there for comedy and a good time. We found our way, on a drizzly evening, through a maze of cobbled streets and endless drinking tents to a tiny venue in a damp stone basement to see Claudia's adorably quirky show (which ended up being nominated as one of the six best shows of the Fringe). I discovered that the Edinburgh Military Tattoo was also on and managed to finagle a single ticket half an hour before it started, run up the Royal Mile to the castle and join the thousands in the stands. There's nothing quite like the swirl of kilts and the squeal

Bucolic beauty: TOP *Cat on the fence in the New Forest.* RIGHT *Cascade of roses at Kifsgate, Gloucestershire.*

'EVERYWHERE
YOU GO, THERE
YOU ARE.'

230

TOP *Front row at the cattle judging at the Alresford show.*
ABOVE *Edinburgh Tattoo at the castle.*
LEFT *On the HMS Britannia with Madeleine.*

of the bagpipes to stir one's blood as a massed pipe band emerges from the mist of the ancient gate of Edinburgh castle. (I must be my father's daughter after all. He was a Major in the NSW University Scottish Regiment during my teenage years, which I thought a strange pastime for a scientist.)

While in Edinburgh Mads and I decided to go on a tour that I would never have imagined I'd enjoy, except a cool thirty-something suggested it. We caught a bus out to the seaside and boarded the HMS *Britannia*. The Queen's boat built in 1953 is now a ship museum berthed near Edinburgh, and is a fascinatingly voyeuristic experience. A 1950s microcosm preserved in aspic, one sees the Queen's tiny bedroom with her chaste little single bed, the Royal sun lounge complete with cane chairs and a bar, the officers' mess and living quarters just as they were, operating theatre, laundry galleys – it's a giant wonderful period doll's house. Mads and I spent hours on it exploring nooks and crannies and finished our visit quite appropriately with a cream tea (that most English of customs) as the mist began to swirl around the boat.

Now as I write this it's another summer in Europe. I'm in a cool white-washed room with the cicadas buzzing in the woods, cowbells clonking in the fields below, and a breeze is blowing through the window. I am back in the Cevennes in the tiny village with family. I can hear my sister Sarah and my mother Rae (who is visiting from Sydney) chatting away happily in the next room, while my two lovely nephews and their dad are pottering around next door in their stone tent. If my darling girls were here with me my happiness would be complete. A thunderstorm is brewing in the forest-clad mountains that appear to fade layer on layer from green to blue into the misty distance and it is utterly lovely. The world can be a very beautiful place to be.

TRAVELLING

———

One of the major motivations for living in London is being able to travel for a lot less. London is the hub of low-cost air travel. It is a brilliant hopping-off point for great low-cost airlines that fly all over Europe. It allowed me to travel and meet up with friends in Europe for so little money, and sharing a hotel room kept the costs to a minimum. The best of the budget airlines, as far as I've experienced, is EasyJet and I travel with them whenever I can. For a little extra, you can also pre-book your seat and board first. The downsides? You pay a flat fee for your in-hold luggage and have a limit of 20 kilos. You also pay for any food and drink on board but that's no problem, just buy a readymade snack at Pret a Manger in London or Paul in Paris before you hop on the plane. The upside? Amazing prices, particularly if you buy well in advance. After flying such long distances from Sydney, it is incredible to think that in under a few hours you can be almost anywhere in Europe.

I've always loved train travel, ever since I first travelled in a sleeper from Sydney to Adelaide when I was eight years old. Train journeys, even the ho-hum ones, evoke the old-school romance of travel. The Eurostar is the only way to go to Paris from London. This is not a budget option; however, this fast train takes you from the centre of London to the centre of Paris in just two and a quarter hours, without all the tedious palaver of airports. So there are no costs for schlepping out to the airport. Diana Vreeland once said, 'The best thing about London is Paris', and the Eurostar makes that so possible.

In the summer the Eurostar from London to in the South of France is a dream of a trip, five or so hours, one of my favourites of all. In general, in France the TGV fast trains are efficient, good value and you can get from Paris to Provence in about three hours.

In England, the birthplace of the railway, the train system is ironically a painfully inefficient, complicated and slow network of privately owned companies. Do your research, as the same trip can cost anywhere from 30 to 300 pounds. I've found that ticket offices can help you find the best price and help navigate the complex rules of peak and off-peak travel. The single tickets are almost as expensive as the returns so it pays to get a return ticket and for a little extra, buy a monthly return rather than a day return for flexibility. But for pure delight, take one of the wonderfully restored steam train journeys available such as the Mid Hants Railway's Watercress line, which runs between Alresford and Alton in Hampshire.

SURVIVING LONG-HAUL FLIGHTS

———

At the other end of the spectrum is the big long-haul flight, which I do once a year. My honest-to-god advice is that economy is almost unbearable, so amass points by flying one airline and using a credit card that adds airline miles, and upgrade. When I've run out of points I splurge now and again as I'm working full time, buy premium economy on my credit card and earn points again. My experience on QANTAS has been that it's almost as good as business class: quiet and secluded with great service. It makes the unbearable bearable. I do think long-haul airlines should rethink how they charge. I'd be happy to pay for my food and drink and get a cheaper airfare instead of paying a premium to let other people get sozzled on endless champagne.

No matter what class I fly, this is what makes a better trip and arrival for me. I walk around a lot and regularly do yoga stretches down the back. I drink only water; no alcohol, no fruit juice, no tea and no coffee. (Not a stretch for me as I don't do them in my normal life.) I mainly drink still water as I've heard the bubbles are not that good for you in the air.

I use a rose mist by Janesce (from South Australia) to spray regularly; not only does it smell delicious but it helps hydrate my skin and nose. I use Fess saline nasal spray, which has reduced the nose bleeds I used to get after flying. And I take Jet Ease, homeopathic pills made in New Zealand, when I fly long-haul and it seems to help with the dreaded jet lag. I don't wear makeup and I slather my face with a gentle rose face cream (from Janesce again).

I'm like a budgie; I put a cover over my eyes and fall asleep. I carry a big black cashmere wrap for warmth and wrap it over the top of my head, as I hate those nasty little slippery eye masks they give you on planes. My sister Emma, who lives in Hong Kong, swears by the soft jersey eye masks by Bodas, London. Warm socks are a must as my feet turn to blocks of ice, and I use Falke sensitive wool knee-highs. I use Sennheiser noise-cancelling earpieces as I am allergic to the horrid headsets.

※

WHEN I ARRIVE AT MY DESTINATION

———

Staying in apartments rather than hotels is my preferred option and for this try the Airbnb website, which has changed the way people travel just as Facebook has changed the way people interact.

Learning something and doing something with like-minded people is a great way to have a holiday for a lone traveller, such as a yoga retreat, cooking course or photography workshop.

WHAT I'VE LEARNT ABOUT

PACKING

———

No matter how much I travel, packing is still a tortuous process. But if you love travelling and still want to look good there's no way around it. I've never achieved 'oh, I only take carry-on' status, much as I think it's commendable. Hey, I'm a fashion editor after all and it's the shoe thing. Also, I've discovered if I don't pack what I need I'm likely to buy it while I'm away.

This is how I pack. About a week or so before the trip, long or short, I get out the suitcase suitable for the trip. I have suitcases for different trips, a big long-haul suitcase that is super lightweight in a taupe-coloured fabric that I can recognise on the carousel, a smaller soft suitcase by Lipault, a French brand that makes squishy suitcases you can squeeze into spaces on the train, even when you have to have it pressed against your shins in your seat, and an overnight version by the same brand.

Every time I think of something I throw it in the suitcase. First up: passport, wallet, then lingerie bags of undies, and the clothes just get thrown on top to start. Shoes, I stack beside the case. A day before the journey I actually pack, pulling everything out and starting again, whittling away my choices. I try to stick to a general colour scheme so everything works together. The damn shoes – that's what makes cases so heavy but you need to change shoes often to relieve your feet. So my usual suspects for travel (stashed in cloth bags) include good-looking trainers that you can walk forever in, light ballet flats that can double as slippers, stilettos for dressing up and for summer, flat, comfortable sandals and in winter, warm boots. I use dry-cleaning bags to put my best clothes in as it really reduces crushing, something I've learnt from my styling days. And I hang things as soon as I arrive. My photographer friend Juli Balla told me recently of a tip she learnt in New York from stylist Di Shepherd, of giving your garment a light spray with water and letting it hang for a few minutes.

*

THE LISTING
MY TRAVEL PLACES

———

Here are just some the places I have loved visiting. No guarantee that they'll be as good as I found them. Try checking the hotels with TripAdvisor, which I find very useful, both the listings and the travellers' reviews (often unwittingly hilarious). **www.tripadvisor.com**

Try also Airbnb, a fantastic idea where you rent safely from real people. The site verifies the info, approves or creates the photos of each property and the travellers review the properties and the hosts, in a kind of cross between Facebook, TripAdvisor and eBay. Now almost anywhere in the world you can find a little place to rent. Brilliant! **www.airbnb.com**

'EVERYWHERE YOU GO, THERE YOU ARE.'

236

FRANCE

———

AIX EN PROVENCE
ATELIER PAUL CEZANNE
www.atelier-cezanne.com/anglais
9 avenue Paul Cézanne
13090 Aix en Provence, France
Telephone: +33 (0) 4 42 21 06 53

Step into an artist's world at Cezanne's studio with its long shelf strewn with many of his favourite still life subjects – a vase, a skull, a ginger jar, or a little plaster cupid. A walk up the hill will reveal Mont Sainte Victoire, which he loved to paint. Aix-en-Provence is the city he was born and died in and you can visit other significant places associated with Cezanne on a special tour. Visit the official website at www.aixenprovencetourism.com

GAGO
20 rue Fabro
13100 Aix en Provence, France
Telephone: +33 (0) 4 42 26 08 52

A chic multi-brand boutique of some of the best of the world's fashion-forward labels, which has been trading for decades. Strangely without a website.

HOTEL CARDINAL
www.hotel-cardinal-aix.com
24 rue Cardinale,
13100 Aix en Provence, France
Telephone: +33 (0) 4 42 38 32 30

A charming, slightly shabby hotel, well priced, well situated and full of antiques. I loved my stay here.

HOTEL CEZANNE

www.cezanne.hotelaix.com
40 avenue Victor-Hugo
13100 Aix en Provence, France
Telephone: +33 (0) 4 42 91 11 11

A super modern hotel with an alarmingly lurid foyer. Well appointed though with small rooms and very helpful staff.

ARLES

HOTEL NORD PINUS

www.nordpinus.com
14 Place du Forum
13200 Arles, France
Telephone: +33 (4) 90 93 44 44

Lunch, stay or just have a drink in the bar where bullfighting aficionados such as Ernest Hemingway, Pablo Picasso and Jean Cocteau visited over the years.

L'HOTEL PARTICULIER A ARLES

www.hotel-particulier.com
rue de la Monnaie
13200 Arles, France
Telephone: +33 (0) 4 90 52 51 40

A very chic hotel in a 19th-century mansion. I've visited but not stayed; however, friends who can afford five-star prices did stay there and loved it.

LES RENCONTRES D'ARLES PHOTOGRAPHIE

www.rencontres-arles.com
34 rue du Docteur Fanton
13200 Arles, France
Telephone: +33 (0) 4 90 96 76 06

A brilliant international photographic festival, spread across amazing venues in the mysterious Provençal city of Arles. Each annual festival has a different theme; one year I visited designer Christian Lacroix, originally from Arles, was the guest curator. It is on from June to September annually.

MARSEILLE

LA BAIE DES SINGES

www.la-baie-des-singes.fr
Cap Croisette
13008 Marseille, France
Telephone: +33 (0) 4 91 73 68 87

Eat al fresco in a whitewashed block while sitting on the rocks overlooking the sea.

HOTEL LE CORBUSIER

www.hotellecorbusier.com
280 boulevard Michelet
13008 Marseille, France
Telephone: +33 (0) 4 91 16 78 00

For architecture buffs, a hotel and restaurant in the middle of the modernist block of apartments designed by Le Corbusier.

ST REMY DE PROVENCE

Chateau de Roussan
route de Tarascon
13210 St Remy de Provence, France
Telephone: +33 4 90 90 79 00

A quintessential Provençal experience staying in a charming hotel, more a manor house than a chateau, in the middle of the countryside not far from the pretty town of St Remy.

ITALY

VENICE

LA BIENNALE DI VENEZIA

www.labiennale.org
Ca' Giustinian, San Marco
1364/A 30124 Venice, Italy
Telephone: +39 041 521 8711

An extraordinary biennial feast of contemporary art, to both shock and delight, housed in designated country pavilions in the gardens and in venues all over Venice. It is held every two years (in the years ending in odd numbers) July to November.

CASA MARTINI

www.casamartini.it
Cannaregio 1314
30124 Venice, Italy
Telephone: +39 041 717 512

An atmospheric boutique hotel tucked away in a tiny side street in a fascinating residential area of Venice, a walk away from the main train station.

PALAZZO FORTUNY

fortuny.visitmuve.it
San Marco 3958
30124 Venice, Italy
Telephone: +39 041 520 0995

An evocative crumbling palazzo where designer Mariano Fortuny lived and created his classically inspired pleated gowns and rich velvet Renaissance-style textiles. Also an inspired venue during the Biennale with a magical light installation by James Turrell. This is my favourite place to visit in Venice.

PUNTA DELLA DOGANA

Dorsoduro 2,
Venice, Italy
Telephone: +39 044 523 0313

A centre for contemporary art housed in the magnificent former customs house perched out on the Grand Canal.

SPAIN

BILBAO

GUGGENHEIM BILBAO

www.guggenheim-bilbao.es/en
Avenida Abandoibarra
2 48009 Bilbao, Spain
Telephone: +34 944 35 90 00

An art destination par excellence with monumentally scaled works that envelop you with their power.

MALLORCA

EYE PHOTOGRAPHIC WORKSHOPS

www.eyephotographicworkshops.com

Informative and entertaining photographic workshops by photographer Michael Potter in various lovely locations including his studio in London and his Spanish home in Pollenca, Mallorca.

UNITED KINGDOM

EDINBURGH

THE DOGS

www.thedogsonline.co.uk
110 Hanover St
Edinburgh, Scotland EH2 1DR
Telephone: +44 (0) 131 220 1208

Edinburgh has a cool foodie scene and
this place is hip and the food is great.
Madeleine and I loved its quirkiness
and good, modern Scottish food.

THE FESTIVAL FRINGE

www.edfringe.com

The city buzzes with strange,
extraordinary performers and
events from all over the world.

THE MILITARY TATTOO

www.edintattoo.co.uk
The Tattoo Office
32 Market Street
Edinburgh, Scotland EH1 1QB
Tickets: +44 (0) 13 1225 1188

If you love bagpipes en masse and
swirling tartans, this event in magnificent
Edinburgh castle is a must-do.

GLOUCESTERSHIRE

HIDCOTE MANOR

www.nationaltrust.org.uk
Hidcote Bartrim,
near Chipping Campden,
GL55 6LR, United Kingdom
Telephone: +33 (0) 13 8643 8333

This arts and crafts garden and manor
house is intriguingly divided into
outdoor rooms.

KIFTSGATE COURT GARDENS

www.kiftsgate.co.uk
Chipping Campden
Gloucestershire GL55 6LN,
United Kingdom
Telephone: +44 (0) 13 8643 8777

A private garden open in the summer
with magnificent rose gardens
surrounding a neo-classical house.

SEZINCOTE HOUSE

Near Moreton-in-Marsh
Gloucestershire
GL56 9AW
Telephone: +44 (0) 13 8670 0444
www.sezincote.co.uk
www.nationaltrust.org.uk

A Mughal-inspired folly of a place built
in the early 19th century where you can
visit both house and garden.

PENZANCE

THE ABBEY HOTEL

www.theabbeyonline.co.uk
Abbey Street
Penzance, Cornwall TR18 4AR,
United Kingdom
Telephone: +44 (0) 17 3636 6906

The delightful neo-Gothic building
housing The Abbey Hotel is owned
by iconic sixties model Jean Shrimpton
and her husband.

ABOVE

Home sweet home:
My sitting room in Winchester,
with a view through the
Georgian windows.

RIGHT

The purple door.
Photos: Polly Eltes

CHAPTER EIGHT

Becoming
JANE

Home at last

The church bells are pealing in joyous carolling across the tree-lined cathedral square and the sun is streaming through my Georgian floor-to-ceiling windows of the most beautiful proportions, and here I am at home in Winchester in Hampshire, England. How did I come to be here?

One early morning in London – another one of my reflection times – I was thinking about my purpose in life and what gives it meaning. I have these existential examinations of my life early in the morning while I'm lying in bed. Maybe because I've been meditating (the empty space in your head seems to clarify things) or I've been reading something that inspires me. My musings went on and it became clear that it was time to make a new plan for the future. In so many ways what I had envisaged for my life when I left Australia had been realised. Now it was time to see where I wanted to go next and how I would spend the next five years of living. Not in some ghastly corporate mission statement way, but rather creating it by letting my mind travel and then realising it all in a beautifully visual way. I decided that if I could visualise it, I believed it would happen. Making the vision boards (detailed in chapter six) was an important part of the process. When I finished the boards I was surprised by the final imagery. Here was I thinking I was the ultimate urban girl who loved living in the heart of this fantastic big city, yet I had created a page covered with images of green trees, old manor houses surrounded by fields and Georgian houses with gardens filled with flowers.

Aside from my dreams, there was the very pragmatic imperative of actually earning enough to live on. Along with writing and styling freelance, I'd been lecturing at university for some years. What began as a request from Clementine to do a little bit of teaching in the fashion styling degree gradually became a much bigger commitment over the few years since I had started. Each year I've ended up doing more teaching and, almost by stealth, my hours and commitment had increased. As the university was in Southampton I had to travel by

University life: TOP *Me and
Elizabeth in academic robes.*
CENTRE LEFT *Chic Sharon
on our way to the V&A to see Tom
Ford.* CENTRE RIGHT *With
Kathy Lette and Dannii Minogue,
both awarded honorary doctorates
by Southampton Solent University.*
LEFT *Clementine, Elizabeth and
Jennifer at exhibition opening.*

Winchester wonders:

TOP
*View of the square during
the Queen's Jubilee.*

BELOW
*Flower festival at
Winchester Cathedral.*

train to and from London. Early mornings at Waterloo Station became a weekly event; the train hurtling through the outer reaches of London and on into green fields. When the train approached Winchester it seemed particularly beautiful and I would look down from the train window and think how lovely the town looked.

When Clementine and Jennifer, the beautiful and clever course leader, sat me down one day, looked at me eagerly, both saying, 'If we could get a full-time position created, would you be interested in applying for the job?' I found myself saying, 'Yes, sure!' It took a while but eventually the job was created and the interviews happened. Eeek! I hadn't applied for a job in years as they have always materialised out of the ether. I sat in front of a panel of four people and was alarmed to find that I was actually feeling nervous. In the middle of the interview I had a coughing fit, which I am prone to, and had to rush out of the room, choking and struggling to breathe for what seemed like ages. Before you have visions of me coughing into a lace hanky, expiring in the sterile corridor and losing the opportunity to take on my new life challenge – I got the job.

When I first started working there, I was shocked at the new students, at how little they knew and how poorly educated they were. But gradually I fell in love with them all and came to know their faces, their quirky, individual dress sense, their varying regional accents, and their talent and potential.

'Who is your favourite fashion photographer?' I asked in one of my first tutorial sessions a year or so ago. Twenty-five pairs of eyes looked at me blankly. 'Surely you've heard of one famous fashion photographer?' I asked, shocked. 'Aren't you wanting to be fashion stylists?'

One person finally answered, 'Mario Testino' and I breathed a little easier and then this cheeky lad with a lilting Welsh accent said, 'You know in that movie *Devil Wears Prada* where she says, "Get me Patrick on the phone". Well . . . him . . . Patrick.'

'Ah,' I said, 'That would be Patrick Demarchelier. You know

I once worked with him when we were shooting Nicole Kidman.' Those twenty-five pairs of eyes widened and I knew that I had their attention. I realised at that point that I could make some kind of impact teaching them.

And there it is, a perfect purpose for me at this stage of my life. It feels rather cheesy to say this but I believe I can make a difference to their lives, I can pass on what I know and I can help them get a job. With the considerable advantage of a comfortable middle-class life, a very good education and a fantastic career, I can give something back. Before we crack out the violins, you should see me in the middle of marking endless papers or struggling with the endless tedious bureaucracy and hear the expletives issuing from my mouth.

So I found myself extricating myself from my busy London life to move to the country, to Winchester – one of the prettiest country towns in England, a historic old town, full of beautiful Georgian houses and the most beautiful Gothic cathedral, surrounded by rolling green fields. Clementine took me to Winchester one day and we had afternoon tea at a cute little teahouse called 'Ginger for Two' and I remember thinking, 'I could live right here'. I trawled through the real estate listings and spied a place that had the same outlook as my flat in London, right in the heart of Winchester overlooking a square. There was a feeling in my gut that this was the place for me. The real estate agent tried to fob me off with 'We can't show it to you at present as the ceiling upstairs has fallen in and the workmen are in the midst of repairs.' But I knew it was going to be mine, so I insisted: 'I would like to see it now, I have little time to view and the work won't put me off if I can see its potential.' I was dogged in my pursuit. We had to go in at the back, down a pokey alley, past garbage bins and then into the flat. When we entered through the lovely violet painted door I felt my heart skip a beat. There were two floor-to-ceiling Georgian windows in the sitting room flooding the empty room with light, which looked out onto the square. I was completely smitten. Even standing under the

TOP *Ancient buildings in the cathedral close.*
CENTRE LEFT *Medieval tiles on the cathedral floor.*
CENTRE RIGHT *Gateway to the close.*
LEFT *Shopping mecca, the Hambledon.*

TOP *Burne-Jones stained glass in the cathedral.*
BOTTOM *Me in the archways.*

gaping hole in the bedroom ceiling didn't dampen the feeling.

I walked over to Winchester Cathedral, just across the square, through a glowing green alley of trees, and wandered into its cool depths. It has such a palpable sense of a spiritual life and centuries of solace that my breath caught in my throat as I walked over the worn medieval tiles. The cathedral, begun in the 12th century (being from the New World that always seem extraordinary to me), has a sturdily grand Norman section and an ethereally soaring Gothic nave with strange patchwork stained-glass windows. A quintessential older Englishwoman with a posh voice, dressed in an old trench coat, darted through the cathedral giving me a lightning-fast tour and when she showed me where Jane Austen was buried, I just knew I had found my new home. I went back to the real estate agent and took the place on the spot.

The day I moved in I was utterly charmed. Through my windows I looked out to see Union Jack bunting strung across the streets for the Diamond Jubilee. It was fluttering in the breeze and a woman was crouched down painting the bollard in the square below me with a Kandinsky! On all the bollards along the square she had painted famous works of art – a Picasso here, a Matisse there, a Gustave Klimt further down. *I must be in the right place*, I texted my friend Susan, *There's a woman painting a Kandinsky on a bollard right below me*. I felt like I'd stumbled onto some charming film set.

What I love about my place is that as I face onto the square, life is all around me (I've managed to replicate my London flat's ambience very nicely). And even better, The Hambledon, the best shop in the whole of Winchester with clothes and beauty products, is right next-door. All in all, I have found a little piece of paradise. Perfect – aside from the noise. During the day there's the dull rumble of tourist groups passing or the crash and tinkle of eating and conversation in the cafés below, all lively and just fine, at night it is another matter. The pounding issuing from the ridiculously named 'The Slug and Lettuce' next door,

*Becoming Jane: My home, decorated with auction finds
and Sarah's painting on the mantelpiece.*
Photo: Polly Eltes

which cranks up late at night with a cacophony of thumping music and cackling kids smoking below my windows is excruciating. Mercifully, double-glazing in my bedroom helps a lot and somehow I have become used to it and seem to sleep through the noise most nights.

Though it was the middle of summer when I moved in, the rain poured down day after day. It was a monsoonal downpour of epic proportions. The day of the Hat Fair was no exception. This is a crazy event that happens every year in Winchester and draws street performers from around the world. It materialised, despite the constant rain, in the square below me. I heard the dulcet tones of an Australian girl as she juggled and joked, drawing in the audience, and a Spanish guy performed feats of balance in the pouring rain as the bright brollies clustered around him. I was entertained as I unpacked endless boxes and dropped a donation out the window and down to the Aussie as she passed by. While it rained incessantly, indoors I played house, spreading out into the gorgeous two floors of space. I had, for the first time in years, a proper bedroom, in fact, two bedrooms and am the proud possessor of two loos; a 'cloakroom' as the English term it, downstairs and a bathroom upstairs. Luxury indeed! I took the plunge and bought a proper sofa, a deep, country-house styled piece (where I now sit cross-legged and write), and I feel like a proper grown-up. No more living like a student. This is my home. I feel like Holly Golightly in *Breakfast at Tiffany's* when she finally decides to give the cat a name.

Finally, the sun came out again and this was made more exciting because my daughter Madeleine had come to stay for a month en route to going to live in New York. She has perfect timing and seems to have a knack of coming just as I start a new life and always helps me smooth out the bumpy bits. My other daughter Emily talked to us on Skype, as she does with me nearly every day, and it felt as if we were all together again. (Though Emily has visited me in Paris and London, she is still to come to Winchester.) Mads and I went to Winchester Cathedral and lit candles for the three of us. We looked at Jane Austen's memorial where she was buried after she died in a shabby little house still standing just near the College on 18 July 1817. To a bemused Mads I insisted that we must go to Evensong in the Cathedral. I think she must have been wondering what had happened to her Buddhist mama. But there in the cathedral on a chilly evening as the glorious hymns soared into the arches, sung by the boys and men that make up the incredible choir, I could see she understood.

'Are you from East Grinstead? the stately Dean greeted us as we left. 'No, we're from Australia,' Mads told him proudly.

'Ah,' he said, looking slightly bewildered. 'Well, welcome.'

I think we crashed a special service for the happy inhabitants of that village, wherever it may be.

Mads and I started exploring the town surrounds; we walked for miles every day across the water meadows, where the green streams gushed with trailing long green tendrils through the crystal clear torrent and I could see daisy-like flowers underwater. It reminded me of the beautiful pre-Raphaelite painting of Ophelia and I can see it was not some fanciful rendering by Millais of an idyllic landscape for poor drowned Ophelia, but an accurate depiction of an English country stream. We marvelled as a white swan glided by with seven almost fully grown brown cygnets following in her wake. We walked across the moors on a raised wooden walkway above the water, listened to the rustlings in the reeds and saw a little brown furry thing swimming across the stream. A critter at last – we were looking for otters or moles but to no avail so Mads bought a card with a mole in spectacles and stuck it in the bushes for me. At one point Mads laughed and said that she never thought she would hear me utter the words, 'What a beautiful dry wall!' She continued to be very amused by me constantly waxing lyrical about the landscape. Isn't this the person she could barely prise out of shops, who usually effuses about a gorgeous dress or a divine handbag? Ah yes it is, but somehow looking at this 'green and pleasant land' fills me with joy.

On a hot day we sunbaked in the meadows, dangled our feet in the freezing river and walked to The Hospital of St Cross, the wonderful medieval abbey with the most beautiful enclosed garden. For hundreds of years it has provided a home for elderly brothers and food for the poor. To give it its full name it is called evocatively 'Almshouse of Noble Poverty'. If one is going to be poor, what could be better than the notion of 'noble poverty'? You can still request a 'wayfarers' dole' – bread and ale. I did and then felt obliged to drink the warm, disgusting flat brown ale and eat the dry piece of white sandwich bread that was proffered. I remember walking home; Mads was wearing a crazy foldable hat with bobbles all around it and a gentleman walking his dogs said, 'Oh, it's the Winchester Riviera look.' We all laughed as we passed by. We walked to the ice-cream van at the end of the meadows where I've taken to getting an ice-cream each day and Mads deadpanned to the ice-cream man, 'I am going to New York and once I'm gone if my mother comes too often, can you please refuse service.'

Every day I feel I'm becoming Jane, stepping into her landscape and the life of one of her delicious novels. On my search for Jane Austen, Mads and I drove to the village of Chawton where Jane lived for many years with her sister Cassandra and mother, and where, on a tiny table on which you could barely balance a plate, she wrote and revised her famous novels. The village is so charming with a cluster of thatched houses surrounding the sweet cottage where Austen lived. One can just imagine the two sisters walking through the village and around the countryside. *Pride and Prejudice* springs to life before me. I can almost see Elizabeth and Jane Bennett walking by. A thunderstorm approached as we were walking through the village and a solicitous policeman suggested we find cover before the rain came, bless him. If he'd appeared in the dashing red coat of a Regency officer, I don't think I would have been surprised. During the storm, we sheltered in Jane's very own house with a mantelpiece exactly like the one in my sitting

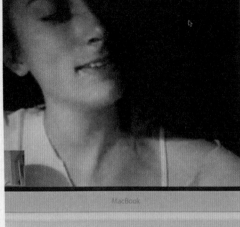

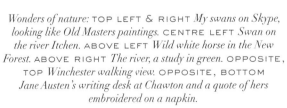

Wonders of nature: TOP LEFT & RIGHT *My swans on Skype,
looking like Old Masters paintings.* CENTRE LEFT *Swan on
the river Itchen.* ABOVE LEFT *Wild white horse in the New
Forest.* ABOVE RIGHT *The river, a study in green.* OPPOSITE,
TOP *Winchester walking view.* OPPOSITE, BOTTOM
*Jane Austen's writing desk at Chawton and a quote of hers
embroidered on a napkin.*

Why not seize the pleasure
at once? How often is
happiness destroyed by preparation,
foolish preparation.

Jane Austen

room and I felt a lump in my throat at seeing her little bedroom and reading the moving and loving letter her sister wrote on the death of her beloved Jane. Outside, as we came out when the storm has passed, the sun shone again, the birds sang and the thatched roofs steamed in the sunlight.

One evening for Mads' birthday, I bought tickets for Shakespeare's *As You Like It* to be performed outdoors under the spreading oak trees of Winchester College. The college, which has been educating boys continuously for 600 years, was on summer break. It was an unusually balmy evening and we packed a picnic and sat on our picnic rug on the shiny green lawn and consumed our prosciutto and olive flatbread supper. As dusk fell, we moved to sit in the little amphitheatre and watched the play unfold under the magnificent trees, the stream babbling behind. Mercifully, this was a traditional rendition of the play not some modernised travesty in sneakers and jeans, and the actors looked utterly perfect in their Renaissance garb strolling about the grounds, the stone walls of the College glowing in the lights, as they acted, sang and danced. The convoluted plot made sense and its ridiculously convenient ending seemed perfectly plausible in such pleasant surrounds.

Another evening we went to a quaint pub called the Wykeham Arms, which was decked out with flower-filled baskets, named after the founder of the college William Wykeham. It was Madeleine's birthday and we decided to eat in the dining room with Clementine, surrounded by paintings, etchings and all manner of memorabilia. All too soon the summer drew to an end and Mads flew the coop for New York. I felt sad although her departure gave me the time I needed to write this book! So I braced myself to get disciplined and get down to it. To inspire me to get the writing flowing I summoned up the muse of my heroine Jane Austen. A lady writer in her Hampshire home! How I wish I had her incredible facility with words.

Country life: TOP *The quintessential English pub –*
The Wykeham Arms, Winchester. LEFT *Apple-green.*
ABOVE *Madeleine on Alresford River walk.*

The days draw in, darkness comes earlier and the days are filled with teaching at university and slogging back and forwards from home to Southampton. I can remember standing on the railway station shivering in a quilted parka, fuzzy yellow fur hat (which makes me look like Big Bird from Sesame Street) and some crazy lace-up snow boots and I text Emily: *It's five degrees here*; an immediate text comes back from her saying, *It's thirty here*. The nights are simply freezing and I have the heating cranked up and it's still cold in my sitting room. Upstairs it's warmer and I spend an inordinate amount of time in bed, tucked under my mother's quilt, keeping warm. I can see now why Christmas time is such a big deal here. It is a festive way of making the long winter bearable. Winchester dubs itself 'the Christmas capital of England' and sparkling lights and shimmery decorations are strung up all over the town centre. A huge Christmas tree is placed in the cobbled mall and the Cathedral Close is filled with cutesy wooden huts that house craft shops, all clustered around a big white tent covering an indoor ice skating rink. Just before Christmas, I fly home to Sydney for my wonderful summer fix of family and festivities. Just in the nick of time before I contract a full-blown case of SAD (Seasonal Affected Disorder). I fly back into London and it begins to snow all the way back to Winchester. George calls me and says, 'You had better come straight here on the way otherwise you are going to freeze to death at your place.' I plough up the hill through the snow to his house as the taxi cannot make it up the steep snowy incline and there are families throwing snowballs and making snowmen on the street. 'Where have you come from?' one mother asks, looking surprised at me dragging a suitcase through the snow. 'Sydney' I say. The news is relayed up and down the street. 'This woman has come from Australia!' From thirty degrees to minus one in the space of a day! Inside his house I look out in wonder at the snowy landscape of his backyard. 'It's Father Christmas Land!' I exclaim.

Winter wonderland: Winchester Cathedral; Christmas market and snowy walk.

Floral pink: On the walls and in the gardens of Alresford.

I've been here a whole year and after what seems like eight months of winter, summer finally comes again and the skies are blue and trees are shimmering green. Winchester is bathed in wondrous sunshine. The surrounding meadows are filled with wildflowers. There is nothing more miraculous than an English summer. The change of seasons is such a source of wonder. It's a relief to finish up an academic year at university – all the marking and all the tedious form filling and box ticking finally done. I have to admit it has been exhausting teaching full-time every student year of the three-year degree. There have been times when I've thought of giving up, although when you see some of the amazing images the students are producing, it does seem worthwhile. When one of the first-year students comes to see me in my office, at the end of our discussion about an essay he is struggling with, he grins cheekily and says, 'You are not allowed to leave until we have all graduated. Okay?'. I laugh and agree. I'm so relieved though to leave for the summer break and I relish the empty time and the delicious space in my mind so I can revive myself and do the final edit and update on this book. I take a reviving, glamorous break to Paris for my friend Alexandra's birthday, who has organised a group of friends to visit from Australia to celebrate. We visit exhibitions, go shopping, have a fabulous night at the opera at the spectacular gilded Opera Garnier, with its domed ceiling painted by Chagall, and have a grand birthday dinner at Le Meurice. It seems like a delicious relic of my old fashionable life, to be savoured fleetingly but without regret once it is over.

This summer, the most deliciously warm and sunny I have ever experienced in England, my delightful and indomitable eighty-five-year-old mother Rae comes to stay and while I'm writing on the sofa she sits knitting or patchworking contentedly opposite me. It's such an easy companiable feeling and I imagine that's what it must have been like for Jane Austen, writing on that tiny table in her cottage with her mother and sister pottering around somewhere nearby. Images of everyday pleasures are conjured up in my mind and I can see the parallels in many things, except, of course, for that Jane's exceptional talent. I take my mother over to see Austen's grey memorial stone set into the floor of the cathedral, which reads so poignantly:

In memory of Jane Austen, youngest daughter of the late Revd. George Austen, formerly Rector of Steventon in this county. She departed this life on the 18th of July 1817 aged 41 after a long illness . . . The benevolence of her heart, the sweetness of her temper and the extraordinary endowments of her mind obtained the regard of all who knew her and the warmest love of her intimate connections . . .

The 'endowments of her mind' is an oblique reference to her writing, for although she had been published by then it was under the anonymous guise of 'a lady'. It took decades before her writing was recognised and a shiny brass Victorian plaque was set into the wall near her memorial stone in the cathedral to celebrate her talent.

My mama and I go off on a pilgrimage to Austen's home in Chawton and as we round the corner of the house into the garden, are surprised to come across a whole party of people in Regency dress wandering around in bonnets tied and parasols held aloft alongside us. Mr Darcy and Elizabeth Bennett come to life. They are taking part in the 200-year anniversary of the writing of *Pride and Prejudice*. Who cannot marvel at the fabulous gently satirical opening to the novel? 'It is a truth universally acknowledged that a single man in possession of good fortune must be in want of a wife.'

Well, this single woman, not in possession of a good fortune, is not in want of a husband but she is definitely enjoying having a mate. (I refuse to use the word 'boyfriend' as it seems a ridiculous term for a woman of my age to use, 'partner' seems both too presumptuous and business-like and 'lover' just seems to give way too much information.) My mate and my mama meet and get on famously, bonding well with much gentle ribbing of each other about the cricket (the Ashes are on this summer) and their constant teasing of the 'princess', that is, me.

In Memory of
JANE AUSTEN,
youngest daughter of the late
Rev.ᵈ GEORGE AUSTEN,
formerly Rector of Steventon in this County
she departed this Life on the 18ᵗʰ of July 1817,
aged 41, after a long illness supported with
the patience and the hopes of a Christian.

The benevolence of her heart,
the sweetness of her temper, and
the extraordinary endowments of her mind
obtained the regard of all who knew her and
the warmest love of her intimate connections.

Their grief is in proportion to their affection
they know their loss to be irreparable
but in their deepest affliction they are consoled
by a firm though humble hope that her charity,
devotion, faith and purity have rendered
her soul acceptable in the sight of her
REDEEMER.

Jane's village: TOP *A thatched cottage in Chawton.* LEFT *Her moving gravestone on the floor of Winchester Cathedral: 'the benevolence of her heart, the sweetness of her temper and the extraordinary endowments of her mind'.*

Delicious: TOP *My girls in Sydney*
supporting the Mardi Gras festival
in pink raincoats with lamingtons.
RIGHT *Rainbow over Winchester.*

Occasionally I snap, 'Ha ha very funny' at them as they chortle away at my expense, though I'm delighted they get on well. On Skype with my girls, Mum and I chat away as if we are all together at home, like the old days.

In my sunlit sitting room, my mother and I talk a little about my new life and I explain how much I do miss my girls and seeing her all the time, but that I felt compelled to create a new way of living for myself and that this is now my home. Well, for the foreseeable future until the longing to be with them becomes unbearable. She says, 'I can understand why you live here.' And I come across a quote by Diana Vreeland: 'There's only one very good life and that's the life you know you want and you make it yourself', which goes some way to explaining my need to find my own life and a new place in the world.

One glorious day I'm done with writing for the moment, so I put down the computer and look out to the square. The day is beckoning and I decide we must go out for walk. The sky is a dazzling blue, fluffy clouds bank in the distance, the luxuriant grass and the avenue of trees is like a green halo in front of the cathedral. The sun is shining and a cool breeze is blowing as we walk out past the cathedral down by Winchester College and across the water meadows. The cygnets and their mama swan are preening themselves in their nest by the river and all is right with the world.

I spy, in the tiny laneway that runs near my house, a little boy skipping towards the light and he takes one look at the shining square, throw his arms in the air and shouts 'Woohoo!' Then he turns his little bespectacled face up to the sun and sings at the top of his lungs, 'I'm walking on sunshine, woh-oh! I'm walking on sunshine woh-oh! I'm walking on sunshine woh-oh! And don't it feel good?' I feel like I've become truly myself – Jane – and I am walking on sunshine and it does feel good.

I still face the expat dilemma – it never goes away. It lurks somewhere in my soul and when the angst of being away from my children, my hometown and all that this entails (family, friends and familiar places) takes hold of me, this fills me with sadness. My sister Sarah now makes lightning visits from Paris to London and hops on the train to Winchester to stay. After years of not quite understanding each other, it is now an absolute delight to be together as sisters. But as the years go on, the longing to be with my girls does overwhelm me and I can feel the pull to go back home and be a part of their lives in the fullest way. But how to reconcile being with someone in one country and wanting to live, even some of the time, on the other side of the world? An almost insoluble question and a source of sadness that threatens to derail my relationship. Who knows what will happen?

What I did when I walked out of my life nearly six years ago is probably not something many people would do, I suppose. They might imagine doing it but to actually do it is a crazy leap of faith. For me this was fuelled by a strange cocktail of hope and despair. But it was absolutely the right leap to take. Despite all the ups and downs, I would not have missed a moment of what I've learnt on this big adventure on the other side of the world. I know now that I can uproot myself and create a new life for myself. Sometimes you just have to take the journey alone to find yourself. As to what I'm going to do next, who knows? Hope springs eternal.

Family and friends gallery: CLOCKWISE
FROM TOP LEFT *Alexandra Joel at
her birthday dinner in Paris at Le Meurice
2013. Sarah at her exhibition at
Le Boudoir de Marie Victoire Poliakoff,
2013. Three generations: Madeleine, Rae,
me and Emily in Sydney 2014. Christmas
Eve in Sydney: Mama and daughters 2013.*

Vintage joy: On the wonderful heritage station run by Mid Hants railway, who operate
the Watercress Line steam trains. With thanks to all the volunteers who welcomed me.

HAPPINESS

—

As the Dalai Lama says, 'All human beings seek happiness and an end to suffering.' Discovering what makes me happy, wherever I am, is the life path I've been travelling. Ultimately the answer is love . . . and laughter . . . and when all else fails, I find a little Green and Black's sea salt chocolate helps.

*

THE LISTING
PLACES I LOVE TO SHOP IN WINCHESTER

———

The picturesque cobbled high street of Winchester is full of the usual suspects: worth a browse are better quality British brands such as **Hobbs** and **Jigsaw** for clothing, **Laura Ashley** for furniture, **The White Company** for clothing and beautiful bed linen, and for shoes **Clarks** and **Jones the Bootmaker**. There are street markets almost every day for food, crafts and vintage collectibles.

FAB VINTAGE

**www.fabvintage.co.uk
12 Kings Walk Shopping Centre
Winchester, Hampshire, SO23 8AF
Telephone: +44 (0) 1962 809 137**

A crazy emporium of vintage clothing and accessories at the back of a down-at-heel shopping centre.

THE HAMBLEDON

**www.thehambledon.com
10 The Square
Winchester, Hampshire SO23 9ES
Telephone: +44 (0) 1962 890 055**

My favourite place to shop in Winchester, The Hambledon is a charming mini department store for women and men that is housed in a Georgian townhouse right on the square. On the ground floor I find great bits and pieces amongst the interior and travel books, homewares and beauty products (including my must-haves for sensitive skin by English label Ren). Upstairs is a fashion selection that suits the relaxed lifestyle of a country town, with designer collections from around the world.

VINTAGE HOUND

**www.vintagehound.co.uk
23A Southgate Street
Winchester, Hampshire SO23 9EB
Telephone: +44 (0) 1962 808 224**

A sweet little store, run by a young couple with an eco commitment, stocked with well-chosen pieces for women and men.

PLACES I LOVE TO EAT

———

THE CHESIL RECTORY

www.chesilrectory.co.uk
1 Chesil Street
Winchester, Hampshire SO23 0HU
Telephone: +44 (0) 1962 851 555

A fine-dining experience in an ancient
medieval building.

GINGER TWO FOR TEA

www.gingertwofortea.co.uk
28–29 St Thomas Street
Winchester, Hampshire SO23 9HJ
Telephone: +44 (0) 1962 877 733

A cute tearoom with excellent
cakes. This lovely place was my
first introduction to the delights
of Winchester.

LA PLACE

9 Great Minster Street
Winchester, Hampshire SO23 9HA
Telephone: +44 (0) 1962 864 004

With a bar called 'Froggie's Place',
this restaurant serves classic French fare
with a set menu available at lunchtime.
When the weather permits you can
have your drinks in the outdoor seats
at the tables on the square.

THE WYKEHAM ARMS

www.wykehamarmswinchester.co.uk
75 Kingsgate Street
Winchester, Hampshire SO23 9PE
Telephone: +44 (0) 1962 853 834

A quaintly decorated gastropub, with
a restaurant serving modern British
food with some accommodation.

EVENTS IN WINCHESTER

———

THE HAT FAIR

www.hatfair.co.uk

Britain's long-running street
entertainment festival (the name is
taken from the donations you throw in
the hat) occurs every July in the streets,
parks and squares of Winchester,
bringing street performers from all over
the world.

THE WINCHESTER FESTIVAL OF THE ARTS

www.winchesterfestival.co.uk

A cultural festival of music, theatre,
visual arts and literature held in July
in Winchester.

PLACES I LOVE TO GO

The Hospital of St Cross and Almshouse of Noble Poverty

www.stcrosshospital.co.uk
St Cross Road, Winchester
SO23 9SD
Telephone: +44 (0) 1962 878 218

A beautiful medieval complex which houses twenty-five elderly brothers, as it has done for centuries, with a wonderful garden and lovely Norman church set within the water meadows.

Winchester

www.visitwinchester.co.uk

This pretty town was once the capital of old England under King Alfred and is in the county of Hampshire. It is just over an hour's train journey from Waterloo Station, in London.

Winchester Cathedral

www.winchester-cathedral.org.uk

A magnificent cathedral with Norman and Gothic architecture. It is the burial place of Jane Austen and home of the breathtaking 12th-century illuminated Winchester Bible, still so vivid.

Winchester College

www.winchestercollege.org
College Street, Winchester
SO23 9NA
Telephone: +44 (0) 1962 621 100

Founded in the 14th century, this is the longest continuously running school in Britain. Tours are available around the school and grounds and it is fascinating to see where the 'scholars' have studied through the centuries.

Hampshire and surrounds

Hampshire Food Festival

www.hampshirefare.co.uk

Held in July all over Hampshire.

Isle of Wight

Take a ferry ride from Southampton to the Isle of Wight and catch a bus up to Osborne House.

Jane Austen's house, Chawton

www.jane-austens-house-museum.org.uk
Chawton, Alton, Hampshire
GU34 1SD
Telephone: +44 (0) 142 083 262

The charming cottage where Jane Austen lived in the last years of her life and where she wrote and revised many of her fine novels.

Mottisfont Abbey

www.thenationaltrust.org.uk/mottisfont

An ancient abbey decorated in the 1930s high style by Rex Whistler for its owner, society doyenne Maud Russell.

It is now a National Trust property and the gardens are blessed with huge spreading trees, streams and walled areas with English-style herbaceous borders and cascading rose bowers.

Osborne House

www.englishheritage.org/daysout/
properties/osborne/
York Avenue
East Cowes, Isle of Wight PO32 6JX
Telephone: +44 (0) 1983 200 022

Queen Victoria's 19th-century pile, where she spent the summers with her beloved husband Albert and nine children. Owned by English Heritage, who have recently restored the formidable Queen's bathing machine and placed it in situ at her private little beach. It is like a huge wooden caravan and it used to be dragged by horses into the sea so Queen Victoria could bathe in the sea in privacy.

The Pig Brockenhurst

www.thepighotel.com
Beaulieu Road
Brockenhurst, Hampshire
SO42 7QL
Telephone: +44 (0) 1590 622 354

A lovely country house hotel set in the middle of the New Forest, with delicious food harvested from their own kitchen garden or from within a twenty-five-mile radius. You can eat in the conservatory, which has rough-tiled floors, or wander the garden and stay in the smart rooms. Make sure you book ahead.

The Three Tuns

www.the3tunsromsey.co.uk
58 Middlebridge Street
Romsey, Hampshire SO51 8HL
Telephone: +44 (0) 1794 512 639

A country pub with good food owned by the same people who have The Chesil Rectory in Winchester. Named Hampshire Pub of the Year in 2012.

Watercress Line

www.watercressline.co.uk

Mid Hants Railway is a wonderful restored steam train line complete with vintage railway station that you can visit in the pretty Georgian town of Alresford. Tour through Hampshire countryside on a steam train. Special days include the fabulous wartime re-enactment with whole families dressing up in 1940s clothing or Thomas the Tank engine days for kids in summer.

ACKNOWLEDGEMENTS

——

With deep gratitude and love to my tiny tower of strength of a mother Rae de Teliga and to my bright and beautiful daughters Emily and Madeleine Hawcroft, who have made my journey through life truly worth living. With many thanks to my sisters Sarah and Emma de Teliga and Martha Regnault, who have taught me so much. All my larger-than-life family have inspired and challenged me in equal measure. Without my wonderful friends both 'home' and 'away', my life journey would have been very dull and very lonely. They brighten every day and I'm so thankful for them all.

Why tell this story? I owe the existence of this life, travel and style memoir to the people who wanted to know more about my life leap and to the people who encouraged me to tell it. With big thanks to the brilliant publisher Julie Gibbs, whose delightful illustrated books showed me an appealingly visual way to unfold my story. To editor Jody Lee for asking the questions and giving the comments that greatly improved my somewhat faltering efforts. My thanks to those at Lantern – Emily O'Neill, Carol George, Katrina O'Brien and Jocelyn Hungerford – for making the book finally happen.

With special thanks to my daughter Madeleine who read every word along the way (the only person amongst my family and friends that I could bear to do so) and made the perceptive comments and suggestions that made the whole thing seem possible.

And to the sparkling mirage of beauty that has held me in its thrall and spurred me on throughout my life. In the end, though, I have found that the only thing that really gives life meaning is love, in all its myriad forms.

Photo: Juli Balla

INDEX

LANTERN

Published by the Penguin Group
Penguin Group (Australia)
707 Collins Street, Melbourne, Victoria 3008, Australia
(a division of Penguin Australia Pty Ltd)
Penguin Group (USA) Inc.
375 Hudson Street, New York, New York 10014, USA
Penguin Group (Canada)
90 Eglinton Avenue East, Suite 700, Toronto, Canada ON M4P 2Y3
(a division of Penguin Canada Books Inc.)
Penguin Books Ltd
80 Strand, London WC2R 0RL England
Penguin Ireland
25 St Stephen's Green, Dublin 2, Ireland
(a division of Penguin Books Ltd)
Penguin Books India Pvt Ltd
11 Community Centre, Panchsheel Park, New Delhi – 110 017, India
Penguin Group (NZ)
67 Apollo Drive, Rosedale, Auckland 0632, New Zealand
(a division of Penguin New Zealand Pty Ltd)
Penguin Books (South Africa) (Pty) Ltd, Rosebank Office Park, Block D,
181 Jan Smuts Avenue, Parktown North, Johannesburg, 2196, South Africa
Penguin (Beijing) Ltd
7F, Tower B, Jiaming Center, 27 East Third Ring Road North,
Chaoyang District, Beijing 100020, China

Penguin Books Ltd, Registered Offices: 80 Strand, London, WC2R 0RL, England

First published by Penguin Group (Australia), 2014

1 3 5 7 9 10 8 6 4 2

Text copyright © Jane de Teliga 2014.

The moral right of the author has been asserted.

Cover design by Emily O'Neill © Penguin Group (Australia)
Text design by Emily O'Neill © Penguin Group (Australia)
Cover photograph by Juli Balla
Author photograph by Polly Eltes
All other photographs by Jane de Teliga unless stated otherwise.
Photo on p ii by Juli Balla
Photo and collage image on p iv by Polly Eltes
Australian Women's Weekly covers on p 13 reproduced by permission
of the *Australian Women's Weekly*.
Typeset in Janson Text by Post Pre-Press Group, Brisbane, Queensland
Colour separation by Splitting Image Colour Studio, Clayton, Victoria
Printed and bound in China by C & C Offset Printing Co. Ltd.
National Library of Australia
Cataloguing-in-Publication data:

De Teliga, Jane, author.
Running away from home: finding a new life in Paris, London and beyond/Jane de Teliga.
9781921383229 (hardback)
Includes index.
De Teliga, Jane.
Fashion editors – Australia – Biography.
Journalists – Biography.
746.92092

penguin.com.au/lantern